THE
BLACKFEET

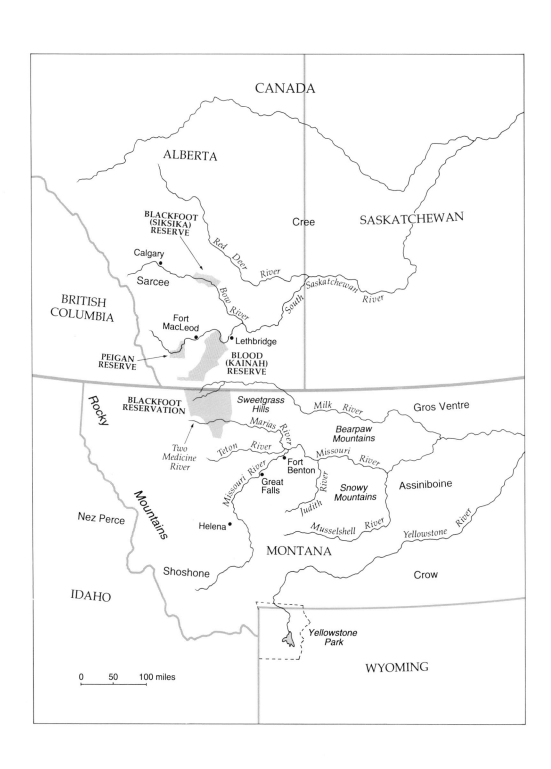

CANADA

ALBERTA

SASKATCHEWAN

Cree

BLACKFOOT
(SIKSIKA)
RESERVE

Calgary

Sarcee

Red Deer River

South Saskatchewan River

BRITISH
COLUMBIA

Bow River

Fort
MacLeod

Lethbridge

PEIGAN
RESERVE

BLOOD
(KAINAH)
RESERVE

BLACKFOOT
RESERVATION

Sweetgrass
Hills

Milk River

Gros Ventre

Rocky

Marias River

Bearpaw
Mountains

Two
Medicine
River

Teton River

Missouri River

Fort
Benton

Missouri River

Great
Falls

Judith River

Snowy
Mountains

Assiniboine

Mountains

Nez Perce

Helena

Musselshell River

Yellowstone River

MONTANA

Shoshone

Crow

IDAHO

Yellowstone
Park

WYOMING

0   50   100 miles

INDIANS OF NORTH AMERICA

THE BLACKFEET

Theresa Jensen Lacey

Frank W. Porter III
General Editor

CHELSEA HOUSE PUBLISHERS
New York   Philadelphia

On the cover   A Blackfeet men's shirt made of hide.

Chelsea House Publishers
Editorial Director   Richard Rennert
Executive Managing Editor   Karyn Gullen Browne
Copy Chief   Robin James
Picture Editor   Adrian G. Allen
Creative Director   Robert Mitchell
Art Director   Joan Ferrigno
Manufacturing Director   Gerald Levine

Indians of North America
Senior Editor   Sean Dolan
Native American Specialist   Jack Miller

Staff for **THE BLACKFEET**
Assistant Editor   Mary B. Sisson
Editorial Assistant   Annie McDonnell
Assistant Designer   Fran Bonamo
Picture Researcher   Sandy Jones

Copyright © 1995 by Chelsea House Publishers, a division of
Main Line Book Co. All rights reserved. Printed and bound
in the United States of America.

First Printing

1   3   5   7   9   8   6   4   2

Library of Congress Cataloging-in-Publication Data

Lacey, Theresa Jensen.
   The Blackfeet / Theresa Jensen Lacey.
      p.   cm.—(Indians of North America)
   Includes bibliographical references and index.
   ISBN 0-7910-1681-1.
      0-7910-2491-1 (pbk.)
   1. Siksika Indians—Juvenile literature.   2. Kainah
Indians—Juvenile literature.   3. Piegan Indians—Juvenile
literature.   [1. Siksika Indians.   2. Kainah
Indians.   3. Piegan Indians.   4. Indians of North
America.]   I. Title.   II. Series: Indians of North America
(Chelsea House Publishers)
E99.S54L33   1995
970.004'973—dc20

94-38594
CIP
AC

CONTENTS

INDIANS OF NORTH AMERICA

CHELSEA HOUSE PUBLISHERS

INDIANS OF NORTH AMERICA: CONFLICT AND SURVIVAL

Frank W. Porter III

The Indians survived our open intention of wiping them out, and since the tide turned they have even weathered our good intentions toward them, which can be much more deadly.

John Steinbeck
America and Americans

When Europeans first reached the North American continent, they found hundreds of tribes occupying a vast and rich country. The newcomers quickly recognized the wealth of natural resources. They were not, however, so quick or willing to recognize the spiritual, cultural, and intellectual riches of the people they called Indians.

The Indians of North America examines the problems that develop when people with different cultures come together. For American Indians, the consequences of their interaction with non-Indian people have been both productive and tragic. The Europeans believed they had "discovered" a "New World," but their religious bigotry, cultural bias, and materialistic world view kept them from appreciating and understanding the people who lived in it. All too often they attempted to change the way of life of the indigenous people. The Spanish conquistadores wanted the Indians as a source of labor. The Christian missionaries, many of whom were English, viewed them as potential converts. French traders and trappers used the Indians as a means to obtain pelts. As Francis Parkman, the 19th-century historian, stated, "Spanish civilization crushed the Indian; English civilization scorned and neglected him; French civilization embraced and cherished him."

Nearly 500 years later, many people think of American Indians as curious vestiges of a distant past, waging a futile war to survive in a Space Age society. Even today, our understanding of the history and culture of American Indians is too often derived from unsympathetic, culturally biased, and inaccurate reports. The American Indian, described and portrayed in thousands of movies, television programs, books, articles, and government studies, has either been raised to the status of the "noble savage" or disparaged as the "wild Indian" who resisted the westward expansion of the American frontier.

Where in this popular view are the real Indians, the human beings and communities whose ancestors can be traced back to ice-age hunters? Where are the creative and indomitable people whose sophisticated technologies used the natural resources to ensure their survival, whose military skill might even have prevented European settlement of North America if not for devastating epidemics and disruption of the ecology? Where are the men and women who are today diligently struggling to assert their legal rights and express once again the value of their heritage?

The various Indian tribes of North America, like people everywhere, have a history that includes population expansion, adaptation to a range of regional environments, trade across wide networks, internal strife, and warfare. This was the reality. Europeans justified their conquests, however, by creating a mythical image of the New World and its native people. In this myth, the New World was a virgin land, waiting for the Europeans. The arrival of Christopher Columbus ended a timeless primitiveness for the original inhabitants.

Also part of this myth was the debate over the origins of the American Indians. Fantastic and diverse answers were proposed by the early explorers, missionairies, and settlers. Some thought that the Indians were descended from the Ten Lost Tribes of Israel, others that they were descended from inhabitants of the lost continent of Atlantis. One writer suggested that the Indians had reached North America in another Noah's ark.

A later myth, perpetrated by many historians, focused on the relentless persecution during the past five centuries until only a scattering of these "primitive" people remained to be herded onto reservations. This view fails to chronicle the overt and covert ways in which the Indians successfully coped with the intruders.

All of these myths presented one-sided interpretations that ignored the complexity of European and American events and policies. All left serious questions unanswered. What were the origins of the American Indians? Where did they come from? How and when did they get to the New World? What was their life—their culture—really like?

In the late 1800s, anthropologists and archaeologists in the Smithsonian Institution's newly created Bureau of American Ethnology in Washington,

D.C., began to study scientifically the history and culture of the Indians of North America. They were motivated by an honest belief that the Indians were on the verge of extinction and that along with them would vanish their languages, religious beliefs, technology, myths, and legends. These men and women went out to visit, study, and record data from as many Indian communities as possible before this information was forever lost.

By this time there was a new myth in the national consciousness. American Indians existed as figures in the American past. They had performed a historical mission. They had challenged white settlers who trekked across the continent. Once conquered, however, they were supposed to accept graciously the way of life of their conquerors.

The reality again was different. American Indians resisted both actively and passively. They refused to lose their unique identity, to be assimilated into white society. Many whites viewed the Indians not only as members of a conquered nation but also as "inferior" and "unequal." The rights of the Indians could be expanded, contracted, or modified as the conquerors saw fit. In every generation, white society asked itself what to do with the American Indians. Their answers have resulted in the twists and turns of federal Indian policy.

There were two general approaches. One way was to raise the Indians to a "higher level" by "civilizing" them. Zealous missionaries considered it their Christian duty to elevate the Indian through conversion and scanty education. The other approach was to ignore the Indians until they disappeared under pressure from the ever-expanding white society. The myth of the "vanishing Indian" gave stronger support to the latter option, helping to justify the taking of the Indians' land.

Prior to the end of the 18th century, there was no national policy on Indians simply because the American nation had not yet come into existence. American Indians similarly did not possess a political or social unity with which to confront the various Europeans. They were not homogeneous. Rather, they were loosely formed bands and tribes, speaking nearly 300 languages and thousands of dialects. The collective identity felt by Indians today is a result of their common experiences of defeat and/or mistreatment at the hands of whites.

During the colonial period, the British crown did not have a coordinated policy toward the Indians of North America. Specific tribes (most notably the Iroquois and the Cherokee) became military and political pawns used by both the crown and the individual colonies. The success of the American Revolution brought no immediate change. When the United States acquired new territory from France and Mexico in the early 19th century, the federal government wanted to open this land to settlement by homesteaders. But the Indian tribes that lived on this land had signed treaties with European governments assuring their title to the land. Now the United States assumed legal responsibility for honoring these treaties.

At first, President Thomas Jefferson believed that the Louisiana Purchase contained sufficient land for both the Indians and the white population. Within a generation, though, it became clear that the Indians would not be allowed to remain. In the 1830s the federal government began to coerce the eastern tribes to sign treaties agreeing to relinquish their ancestral land and move west of the Mississippi River. Whenever these negotiations failed, President Andrew Jackson used the military to remove the Indians. The southeastern tribes, promised food and transportation during their removal to the West, were instead forced to walk the "Trail of Tears." More than 4,000 men, woman, and children died during this forced march. The "removal policy" was successful in opening the land to homesteaders, but it created enormous hardships for the Indians.

By 1871 most of the tribes in the United States had signed treaties ceding most or all of their ancestral land in exchange for reservations and welfare. The treaty terms were intended to bind both parties for all time. But in the General Allotment Act of 1887, the federal government changed its policy again. Now the goal was to make tribal members into individual landowners and farmers, encouraging their absorption into white society. This policy was advantageous to whites who were eager to acquire Indian land, but it proved disastrous for the Indians. One hundred thirty-eight million acres of reservation land were subdivided into tracts of 160, 80, or as little as 40 acres, and allotted tribe members on an individual basis. Land owned in this way was said to have "trust status" and could not be sold. But the surplus land—all Indian land not allotted to individuals—was opened (for sale) to white settlers. Ultimately, more than 90 million acres of land were taken from the Indians by legal and illegal means.

The resulting loss of land was a catastrophe for the Indians. It was necessary to make it illegal for Indians to sell their land to non-Indians. The Indian Reorganization Act of 1934 officially ended the allotment period. Tribes that voted to accept the provisions of this act were reorganized, and an effort was made to purchase land within preexisting reservations to restore an adequate land base.

Ten years later, in 1944, federal Indian policy again shifted. Now the federal government wanted to get out of the "Indian business." In 1953 an act of Congress named specific tribes whose trust status was to be ended "at the earliest possible time." This new law enabled the United States to end unilaterally, whether the Indians wished it or not, the special status that protected the land in Indian tribal reservations. In the 1950s federal Indian policy was to transfer federal responsibility and jurisdiction to state governments, encourage the physical relocation of Indian peoples from reservations to urban areas, and hasten the termination, or extinction, of tribes.

Between 1954 and 1962 Congress passed specific laws authorizing the termination of more than 100 tribal groups. The stated purpose of the termination policy was to ensure the full and complete integration of Indians into American society. However, there is a less benign way to interpret this legislation. Even as termination was being discussed in Congress, 133 separate bills were introduced to permit the transfer of trust land ownership from Indians to non-Indians.

With the Johnson administration in the 1960s the federal government began to reject termination. In the 1970s yet another Indian policy emerged. Known as "self-determination," it favored keeping the protective role of the federal government while increasing tribal participation in, and control of, important areas of local government. In 1983 President Reagan, in a policy statement on Indian affairs, restated the unique "government is government" relationship of the United States with the Indians. However, federal programs since then have moved toward transferring Indian affairs to individual states, which have long desired to gain control of Indian land and resources.

As long as American Indians retain power, land, and resources that are coveted by the states and the federal government, there will continue to be a "clash of cultures," and the issues will be contested in the courts, Congress, the White House, and even in the international human rights community. To give all Americans a greater comprehension of the issues and conflicts involving American Indians today is a major goal of this series. These issues are not easily understood, nor can these conflicts be readily resolved. The study of North American Indian history and culture is a necessary and important step toward that comprehension. All Americans must learn the history of the relations between the Indians and the federal government, recognize the unique legal status of the Indians, and understand the heritage and cultures of the Indians of North America.

A North Peigan watches the setting sun from Lookout Butte in Alberta, Canada. The sun holds a special place in Blackfeet mythology as the creator and nurturer of all things.

THE
COMING
TO
BE
OF
THE
BLACKFEET

Once, a long time ago, the only living thing was Creator Sun, who has been here since time began and will never die. Creator Sun became quite lonely and decided to use his substantial powers to make companions. He spat upon some space dust and made a ball of mud, which became the Earth. From some of the Earth's dust, Creator Sun made a snake, which multiplied itself until there were so many snakes that Creator Sun decided to make the Earth boil and to make lava flow in order to kill the snakes. Only one snake, a female about to bear young, survived.

After this experiment, Creator Sun longed for a mate and decided to create the Moon. Their union was a fruitful one, and the Moon gave birth to seven sons.

Creator Sun and his family were happy until one of the sons of the surviving snake, called Snakeman, changed his form into that of a man and became the Moon's secret love. When Creator Sun discovered the affair he flew into a rage, and he and his seven sons killed Snakeman and the Moon and burned their bodies until all that was left were some ashes.

Despite the Moon's death, Creator Sun realized that she would return somehow to avenge her lover's death, so he prepared his sons for trouble. He gave each of them a tool that they could use to defend themselves against the Moon when she returned. To the youngest son, called Rawman because he was so pink when he was born, Creator Sun gave a bladder of water. The second youngest son was given a bird; the next son, a bladder of air. To the fourth youngest son, the father gave a stick. The fifth was given a small rock; the sixth, some magic powers in his fingers. The eldest son, like Rawman, got a bladder of water.

From the ashes of the fire used to burn the Moon's and Snakeman's bodies, a spark of what was left of the Moon flew out into the sky, and she lived again in her old form. In a murderous rage, she immediately went to her sons' camp to kill her children. The sons ran from her, using the things their father had given them to try and slow her down. The eldest son threw his water bladder at her and caused rain to fall upon her. The sixth son drew a line in the dirt with his finger and created canyons and steep valleys. The son with the rock threw it and made high mountains. The fourth son, who had a stick, threw that down and caused dense forests to grow. The third son threw his bladder of air and made great winds blow all around the Moon. The son with the beautiful, multicolored bird threw it into the air; the bird became the first thunder and lightning. With his bladder of water, Rawman caused a great flood to form around his mother. These obstacles slowed the Moon momentarily, but she continued her pursuit. Just as she reached Rawman, screaming death threats, Creator Sun threw his hatchet at her and cut off her leg. The sons escaped, and the Moon spent four days mending her leg, which was never quite the same again.

The sons and their father became airborne and flew up into the sky. The Moon followed, and they are all still in the sky today. The seven sons became the stars that make up the Big Dipper. They and their father, Creator Sun, are always just ahead of the Moon, and because the seven sons still throw things at the Moon to slow her down, weather of all types comes to the Earth from the sky. In order to hide from the Moon, Creator Sun made day and night. The Moon is kept in the darkness so that she cannot see her sons very well. To punish all the snakes in the world for this trouble, Creator Sun made them to be despised by all others in creation. The Moon was also punished, being left completely bare, with an inhospitable climate and no life forms on her or in her. In addition, Creator Sun caused the Moon to be invisible for several days of the month.

After this disastrous experience with the Moon, Creator Sun decided the Earth would make a better wife. Under the never-ending light of Creator Sun, Mother Earth produced all other life forms. But the snakes who lived on Mother Earth were still hostile to Creator Sun, and some of them changed into huge reptiles and dinosaurs and disobeyed Creator Sun's laws. He destroyed the rebellious animals with a great flood, sparing only the smaller snakes; the remains of these gigantic creatures are excavated by archaeologists today.

Creator Sun then took some mud and made the first man, breathing life into

According to Blackfeet legend, the forests, valleys, mountains, and rivers of their territory were all created by the sons of Creator Sun during their escape from the Moon.

him and calling him Mudman. After a while, Creator Sun noticed that Mudman was lonely. Finding Mudman asleep one day, Creator Sun made Mudman fall into an even deeper sleep, took his smallest rib, and made a woman, Ribwoman, to be his companion. Mudman and Ribwoman began to have children, and they eventually had so many that some of them had to leave and make camps of their own, so that there would be enough food for them all. The children traveled in the four cardinal directions of north, south, east, and west, and they further multiplied, populating the Earth. They spread out so far from one another that their one shared language began to change, becoming many languages. But no matter what language they speak, all humans today are related, being the descendants of Mudman and Ribwoman, and they are all nurtured by the light of Creator Sun, who is everywhere.

Unfortunately, the people were not always well. If they ate the wrong thing by accident, they would become ill, and sometimes, they were in pain. Creator Sun felt bad, seeing so many of his people, especially the children, getting sick and dying. He came to Earth, took Mudman with him into the forests and fields, and showed him the healing powers of certain herbs and barks. He also showed him what saps, berries, and roots he could use for medicine, for both outside and inside the body. Creator Sun taught Mudman how to take sweat baths to purify himself and how to paint his face and body to protect himself from harm.

Creator Sun also taught Mudman how to seek the spirits by going on a vision quest in order to gain power from the spirit world. These instructions were passed on from Mudman to the people, and those who practiced this wisdom became known as medicine men or shamans. Medicine men can never ask for pay in return for healing someone, because it was not Creator Sun's intention that this knowledge be hoarded.

This is one variant of the Blackfeet creation myth. The creation myth was passed on through the telling of stories, and there are numerous modifications of this myth, which often changes from place to place or from generation to generation. Another version of the creation myth states that the first people created were a woman and a child, who were first made of mud and then given the power of speech. The woman immediately began to ask questions, asking the creator what form she and the child were before they were made to live, and then asking him if she and the child would ever stop living. The creator had not yet considered the latter question, so he picked up a buffalo chip (a dried piece of buffalo dung) and told the woman that he would throw it into a lake; if the chip floated, then the people would live forever. The woman was new to life and did not yet know what would and what would not float in water, so she stopped him, pointing out that the buffalo chip would dissolve in the water, and asked him to throw in a stone instead. The stone, of course, sank the instant it was thrown in, and the creator informed the woman that she had just made the decision for all life forms to eventually perish.

This is one of the myths of one of the most powerful Native American tribes still in existence today, the Blackfeet Nation. The Blackfeet Nation includes three divisions: the Siksikas (the Blackfeet proper); the Bloods, or Kainahs (Many Chiefs); and the Pikunis (The Poorly Dressed Ones), Piegans, or Peigans. The traditional territory of the Blackfeet spanned the U.S.-Canadian border, so with the establishment of separate reservations in Canada and the United States, the Peigans were further divided into the Canadian North Peigans and the American South Peigans. The name *blackfeet* came from the color of the soles of the moccasins worn by tribe members; these soles were darkened either with paint or from walking over burnt prairie grasses. It was probably not used to indicate people outside the Siksika division before the arrival of the whites; since the three divisions are culturally and linguistically identical and often fought together as allies, white observers used the name Blackfeet to designate people from all three divisions. Present-day Blackfeet reside in Siksika, Kainah, and Peigan reserves in Alberta, Canada, but the majority now live on the Blackfeet reservation near Browning, Montana.

The history of the Blackfeet, like those of the Native American peoples as a whole, was passed orally from one generation to the next. Because of this oral tradition, stories that are considered

This sketch shows a Blackfeet shaman in ritual attire. Blackfeet myth holds that the medical and spiritual knowledge of such men originated with Creator Sun.

Although the Plains Indians share many elements of their culture, such as horses and tepees, they are not a single homogenous group, but instead are made up of several distinct tribes.

historical by contemporary society are mixed up with stories that are considered mythical. As a result, not much is known about the history of the Blackfeet before they came into contact with the Europeans. There are, however, many theories and explanations as to how the Blackfeet and Native Americans as a whole arrived on the continent of North America.

Most historians and scientists agree that the majority of the Native Americans migrated from Asia. Long ago, a slender thread of land crossed the Bering Sea that separates what is now known as Siberia and Alaska, bringing together the European and North American continents. On a great migration that was to last at least a thousand years, the prehistoric Native Americans traversed the land bridge across the Bering Strait and settled on this continent.

Further evidence in support of this theory was provided in 1991 by a study conducted by a biochemist named Douglas C. Wallace at Emory University in Atlanta, Georgia. Wallace took blood samples from 99 different people from three geographically disparate groups of Indians: the Ticunas of South America, the Mayas of Central America, and the Pimas of North America. Wallace detected rare chemical sequences in the mitochondrial DNA of the samples and found that these sequences occurred only in the DNA of Asian populations. The obvious conclusion is that the Indians occupying the American continent originally came from Asia. Wallace did not find this chemical sequence in Eski-

mos, Navajos, Aleuts, and other tribes who, he theorized, arrived here at a later date. Wallace also claimed that he was able to trace the DNA lineages of these tribes to at least four women in an early migrating group.

On the basis of this shared mitochondrial DNA, Wallace theorized that the Bering Strait trek first occurred 15,000 to 30,000 years ago. There are conflicting hypotheses, however. Geneticist Svante Paabo of the University of California, Berkeley, recently argued against some of Wallace's findings. Paabo claims that the tribes of the Pacific Northwest have 30, rather than 4, different mitochondrial DNA sequences in common, which would place the crossing of the Bering Strait at a much earlier date, 40,000 to 50,000 years ago. Whenever they came, the predecessors of the Native Americans began settling in and multiplying on the continent that is now North America.

From the Bering Strait, the ancestors of the Blackfeet most probably traveled south, then turned east and north. Researchers believe this to be true because the Blackfeet are part of the Algonquin group of tribes, which is a group of linguistically related tribes in North America who inhabited an area ranging from Labrador in the North to the Carolinas in the South to the Great Plains in the West. In addition to being Algonquin, the Blackfeet are one of the group of tribes known as the Plains Indians, which also includes the Sioux, Crows, Kiowas, Arikaras, Pawnees, Nez Perces, Cheyennes, Crees, and Gros

This 1823 etching of the Rocky Mountains portrays the abundant plant and animal life of the Blackfeet's territory.

Ventres. Although they sometimes traded together, often warred against each other, and shared certain elements of their cultures, the Plains Indians are not a culturally homogenous group but are grouped together because they shared a particular geographic area, namely the Great Plains.

Before the advent of the horse, the Blackfeet probably lived on the plains in the northwestern area of what is now the province of Saskatchewan. They were probably hunter-gatherers; unlike some other Plains tribes, there is no indication that the Blackfeet cultivated any crops (except perhaps tobacco) before they discovered horses. Once the horse increased their military capability, the Blackfeet displaced other tribes and settled in the fertile foothills of the Rocky Mountains, in the northwest corner of the Great Plains. The Rockies gave the Blackfeet a natural boundary to their territory and offered them a degree of protection from surprise attacks. The lush hillsides supported plants and trees of all types, such as cedars, spruces, hemlocks, pines, and Douglas firs. The valleys at the base of the mountains had an abundance of rich soil and clear, running streams. But the area also had its haz-

ards; the vast Sea of Grass (as the Blackfeet called the Great Plains) was ruled by quicksilver weather conditions that ranged from raging prairie storms or bone-cracking cold winds to still, hot days that might only be relieved by pounding hailstorms and heart-stopping flash floods. Despite the harsh weather, the wealth and diversity of the land attracted many species of wildlife, many of which are now rare, endangered, or extinct. There were several hundred species of birds, including the red trumpeter swan. The mountains and waters teemed with beaver, mink, deer, and fox, while the plains were covered with enormous herds of buffalo.

Blackfeet territory also contained another form of wealth, one that existed beneath the earth. The Blackfeet did not mine or use metal before the coming of the Europeans and were unaware that their mountains were rich in gold, silver, copper, and coal. Unfortunately, this mineral wealth attracted white settlers and was the determining factor in the U.S. government's decision to restrict the Blackfeet to a reservation only a fraction of the size of the territory they ordinarily traversed in an endless search for plunder and buffalo. ▲

Blackfeet clothing, such as the rawhide coat worn by the center man in this photograph, was most commonly made from buffalo hide. The coat on the right was made from a trading blanket.

SHALL
BE
PEELED
AND
ELK
DOG

Of all the animals who inhabited the fertile plains and foothills of Blackfeet territory, the one that was most important to the survival and lifestyle of the Blackfeet (and the Plains Indians as a whole) was the bison, or buffalo. Before their near extermination by white hunters, the buffalo population in North America numbered in the millions. The enormous beasts ranged from the Rocky Mountains to the eastern woodlands in herds so large that it would sometimes take hours for one to cross a stream. The Blackfeet called the buffalo *eye-i-in-nawhw*, which means "shall be peeled," a reference to the fact that the buffalo was "peeled" (skinned) before it was butchered and eaten.

The buffalo herds were not only a cornerstone of life for the Plains Indians, they symbolized their very existence and freedom and were viewed as a special gift from Creator Sun. According to one Blackfeet legend, Creator Sun, who always kept a watchful eye upon all he had created, saw that the people began to grow thin even though he had given them many different kinds of herbs and other vegetation to eat. He made a four-legged creature from the mud and blew life into the creature's nostrils. Then, as he did with Mudman, Creator Sun caused the animal to fall into a deep sleep. He removed the small rib from the animal and made a mate for it, thus creating the first male and female buffalo. The people began to fill out when they had this "flesh food," or meat, to eat. Creator Sun then made all the other animals: animals and birds to be eaten and animals and birds of prey. The former were to give the people food; the latter, to keep the former's population at a manageable level. Creator Sun also told the Blackfeet that if they would use all they could from each edible animal, and not ever waste, then they would never go hungry again.

For the Blackfeet and other Plains tribes, the buffalo was tangible proof that their creator provided and cared for them, because the buffalo supplied them with virtually everything they needed. The Blackfeet wasted no part of the buffalo; since it was a divine gift, to waste it would not only be foolish but would be a sign of ingratitude to their creator. Each part of the animal had a use, and often more than one. For example, the hide could be scraped clean and tanned with a mixture of buffalo brains, liver, and fat, and used to make robes, caps, leggings, shirts, coats, dresses, belts, moccasins, breechcloths, underwear (made from soft calfskin), and an envelope-like bag called a parfleche used to carry dried foodstuffs. Hides with the hair left on were useful in making winter clothing, and hides that were waterproofed by being smoked over a fire made durable tepees. Rawhide became tools such as pole hitches, horseshoes, blankets, and shields. Hair was used for stuffing pillows, padding saddles, and making ropes, headdresses, and ornaments. Horns made headdress ornaments, masks that protected horses in battle, powder flasks, spoons, cups, ladles, and ceremonial rattles, while bones were made into gaming dice, arrowheads, hide scrapers, knives, and sewing awls. Tendons made fine thread

for sewing clothing and tepee covers and could be used to make strings for bows. The four-chambered stomach lining was cut up to make shoes or clothing or was kept whole and used as a cooking vessel or a water bag. Hooves were made into rattles and glue, and even buffalo chips were used to fuel fires.

Everything edible on the buffalo was consumed. The hump and tongue of the animal were considered delicacies, and the liver was often eaten immediately after making a kill. Tougher parts of the animal were cut in strips and dried to make jerky; this jerky could be ground with stones and mixed with berries and buffalo fat to make pemmican, a lightweight food that resisted spoilage and was used during voyages or when fresh meat was not available.

Since the buffalo was so essential to Blackfeet life, Blackfeet hunters carefully studied its life cycle. The Blackfeet called buffalo of different ages and sexes by different names; for example, a six-year-old, fully mature female buffalo was called "Big Female," while a six-year-old bull was called "Horns Not Cracked," because his horns were usually polished and smooth. The age of the buffalo determined its use, and sometimes whether it was to be killed at all. Older buffalo tended to have tough meat and tough, wrinkled, battered hides, and consequently they were usually left alone. In contrast, calves had distinctive yellow or reddish hair for several months after birth, so their hides were harvested to make children's robes. But the best hides came from the four-year-

Gigantic herds of buffalo roamed the American Great Plains until the late 1800s, when they were almost wiped out by hunters. The destruction of these herds resulted in the loss of an important source of food for the Plains Indians.

Two Plains Indians, disguised as wolves, sneak up to a group of buffalo in this 1851 wood engraving. Before the advent of the horse, the Blackfeet devised numerous ingenious methods for hunting buffalo.

old calves, who were hunted in January and February, when their hair was very silky and thick, like fine fur.

But the buffalo was not simply valued as a source of food and clothing. Children of promise were given names containing the word for buffalo in them, and if a warrior or hunter had brought great honor to his people, his name would be changed to include the word for buffalo. Much of Blackfeet religion centered around the buffalo; medicine men prayed to the buffalo as the intermediary between themselves and the creator, and many items used in religious ceremonies, from masks and headdresses to ceremonial rattles, were made from buffalo parts. Buffalo skulls were used in almost all important religious ceremonies, and medicine bundles, used to cast spells or for personal protection, always included some part of the buffalo.

Blackfeet holy men had several rites for enticing buffalo to come near the hunting camps, since before the horse, buffalo herds had to be within walking distance of a camp in order to be hunted. In one, a holy man who owned a unique stone that was called a buffalo stone because of its shape would hold a ceremony in his tepee along with a number of hunters of renown and would call the buffalo using the magical stone. Buffalo hairballs found on the prairie were also used in ceremonies to attract the animals, as were special songs. Holy men would also have dreams or hold esoteric rituals that would tell them where the buffalo could be found. The Blackfeet

also used a less spiritual method to attract buffalo: each spring they burned old, tough prairie grass to encourage the growth of tender, tasty, new grass.

Once a herd was discovered by scouts, a well-organized hunting party set out after them. Certain young hunters were given the special task (considered a great honor) of providing meat for someone who had no provider, such as a widowed woman and her children or elders who could not hunt for themselves. The hunting party was followed by the women and children, who carried the implements necessary to dress and transport the kill. Since at the slightest sign of danger a herd of buffalo will stampede, often not stopping until miles away, the Blackfeet had strict rules on how the hunt should proceed. Most important, no one was allowed to hunt alone, because although one or two hunters might bring down a couple of buffalo, in doing so they would frighten away the rest of the herd, and driving away game was considered criminal. Discipline during the hunt was so important that a small band of Blackfeet would be deployed to keep the hunt in good order and observe the activities of the actual hunters. The hunters would stalk the buffalo, sneaking quietly up to a chosen beast and killing it with arrows. The hunters would decorate their arrowheads with an identifying design so that the women butchering the buffalo could accurately identify what kill belonged to whom.

Often hunters camouflaged themselves with wolf skins when stalking buffalo; buffalo, being much larger than wolves, are not afraid of them, and the disguised hunters could creep up to a herd without causing a stampede. Hunters discarded their bows and arrows for another type of stalking where they would don buffalo skins, stand next to a cliff, and imitate a buffalo's call—usually that of a buffalo cow. The buffalo, who have very poor eyesight, would follow the call and could be easily lured over the cliff's edge. If there was a large herd of buffalo near a cliff, their tendency to stampede could be used against them. The entire tribe would gather quietly downwind from a herd. On a given signal, they would shout and wave cloths or flaming torches to alarm the herd and cause them to stampede over the edge to their deaths. If any buf-falos survived the fall, they were dispatched by hunters with lances waiting below. When lakes would freeze in winter, the Blackfeet would sometimes drive the buffalo onto the ice. Their weight would break the ice, and the hapless animals would founder in the cold water. Even if the buffalo did not break through the ice, they were not surefooted enough to remain standing for long. Either way, they were easy to finish off with lances, or later, guns.

Because of the migratory nature of the buffalo, travel was a central aspect of Blackfeet life. The Blackfeet never established permanent villages, using camps instead, and everything they made or owned could be quickly packed and easily carried. Their homes, tentlike structures called tepees, were light-

A modern version of a dog travois. Dogs were domesticated by the Blackfeet long before the introduction of the horse to North America.

This painting by Frederic Remington depicts a group of Plains Indians and their horses observing a prairie fire. Horses were valued for their strength, speed, and agility, and they soon became an essential part of Blackfeet life.

weight and could be assembled, disassembled, and carried with relative ease. Tepees had frames made of long wooden poles and walls made of waterproof buffalo skins. When one was dismantled for travel, the tepee was lashed to a sledlike vehicle called a travois, which also carried the Blackfeet's possessions. Originally, these travois were pulled by dogs (which were considered more as work animals than pets), but since a dog could only carry about 50 pounds or pull about 75 pounds, people usually had to carry a part of the load themselves. In addition, young children had to be carried by an adult or had to walk, which slowed progress on the trail.

All this changed with the introduction of the horse to the Blackfeet. Indeed, the horse, called Big Dog or Elk Dog, had an impact on Blackfeet life that was almost as profound as that of the buffalo. Although most historians agree that the horse was introduced to North America by Spanish conquistadores, the Blackfeet have their own explanation. According to Blackfeet myth, the horse was brought to the Blackfeet by a brave named Long Arrow. Long Arrow was an orphan and was for a long time the scorn of his tribe. Finally, his chief, Good Running, took pity on him and adopted him. He matured into a handsome brave and became a fine hunter, but he always remained troubled by the fact that the tribe remembered him as an outcast. Long Arrow decided to do something of

Even with horses, buffalo hunting was dangerous work, as this painting by Charles M. Russell demonstrates. In addition to the hazards posed by the buffalo themselves, parties engaged in a hunt were prime targets for sneak attacks by hostile tribes.

such importance that his people would forget the time when they scorned him and would remember only the great things he did.

When he discussed this decision with Good Running, the chief told him of a legendary spirit tribe who was said to live in the bottom of a lake far away and to keep strange animals who were larger than elk but who worked for people, like dogs. These animals were called *pono-kamita*, or Elk Dogs. Good Running told Long Arrow that many generations of young warriors had gone in search of these Elk Dogs, but none of them had ever come back. Long Arrow decided he would go and try to find them.

The people of the tribe prepared Long Arrow for his dangerous mission. First he was purified by a sweat bath (a religious ceremony wherein individuals congregated to pray and meditate in a heated lodge filled with steam), then he learned how to use a pipe and was taught useful prayers. A shaman gave him "medicine" (a sort of good luck charm) and a painted shield, which had designs on it to protect him. Good Running gave his son his own bow and one final sweat bath before Long Arrow left early one morning.

Long Arrow traveled south until he came to a pond. The spirit of the pond appeared in the shape of a man. He told Long Arrow that he might find the Elk Dogs if he would speak with the spirit's uncle, who lived in a large lake 4 times 4 days' journey away. (Four is a sacred number among many Plains tribes.) Long Arrow walked south for 16 more days, through rough terrain and in bad weather, dry and cold. He finally came to a large lake and found himself facing a spirit-man twice the height of a normal man. The tall spirit menaced Long Arrow, but the young brave showed himself to be unafraid, and the tall spirit decided to help him, telling him to find the grandfather-spirit, who was yet another 4 times 4 days' worth of travel away.

At the end of this time, Long Arrow came to a lake of fantastic size, with snowcapped mountains ringing it. He knew that he must be in the right place and was so exhausted that he collapsed into a deep sleep. He awoke to find a small, beautifully dressed boy standing beside him. The boy told Long Arrow to get up and to follow him down to the bottom of the lake. Long Arrow did so, and found that not only could he breathe underwater, he did not even get wet.

Long Arrow followed the boy to the bottom of the lake, where he found a tepee. Inside the tepee, Long Arrow met the boy's grandfather, who was very powerful and magical. After eating with Long Arrow, sharing a pipe, and praying together, the old man had his grandson show Long Arrow the Elk Dogs. The boy taught Long Arrow how to ride an Elk Dog, and the young brave discovered the exhilaration of riding on the back of one of the beautiful, swift, sleek animals.

Before going back in the tepee, the boy told Long Arrow that if he could catch a glimpse of the old man's feet, then he could ask for a gift. Some days later, Long Arrow managed to see the feet of the old man, which were not really feet at all, but hooves like those of the Elk Dog. When he realized that Long Arrow had seen his feet, the old man granted him three wishes. Long Arrow asked for the old man's multicolored belt, his black medicine robe, and his Elk Dogs.

The old man gave him all he asked for, including half of his herd of Elk Dogs. The old man also told him that the belt and the robe had special powers: the robe would help him to sneak up on and catch the Elk Dogs, while the belt would reveal their songs and prayers, so Long Arrow could learn more about their nature. The old man also gave Long Arrow a magic rope, with which he could always catch any Elk Dog he wanted. Long Arrow returned to his village with the Elk Dogs, finally a hero.

Long Arrow certainly deserved the honor, for the horse made just about every aspect of Blackfeet life easier and more productive. Indeed, the horse bettered the lives of all the Plains tribes, who took to life with the horse as if they had been born to it. The introduction of the horse drastically increased the success of Blackfeet buffalo hunts. Blackfeet scouts could cover a much larger area in their search for bison, and Blackfeet hunters could easily travel long distances and reach distant herds.

Horses made the buffalo hunt itself easier and safer, although it remained dangerous—an average mature bull bison weighs about 2,000 pounds, stands six feet tall at the chest, has two sharp, curved horns, and becomes even more dangerous when frightened or wounded. A hunting party on horses, armed with arrows and lances, could get close to a herd and surround a group of buffalo. When the frightened buffalos tried to flee, a few of the bravest hunters would drive their horses into the center of the fray, then each would ride up alongside a chosen buffalo and, using their lances, arrows, or later, guns, would puncture its diaphragm, heart, or lungs. Often a buffalo had to be struck several times before finally going down; a healthy bison could kill horses, gore hunters, and then run for a mile, all after being fatally wounded.

The Blackfeet could also pack and haul a much heavier load on the horses than they could on the dogs. A larger pack animal meant a family could have a larger tepee and more possessions. The Blackfeet also made a cagelike structure from bentwood and mounted it atop the travois so that the horses could carry children. This made their migrations much faster, which in turn made it much easier for them to follow the bison herds or escape from enemies or natural disasters.

The horse changed Blackfeet society as well. Well-trained horses that could quietly stalk prey or an enemy, could maintain a gallop for long distances, and would remain calm in battle and in the hunt were extremely valuable. As a result, wealth began to be determined by the number of horses one owned, and horses began to be used as dowries or bride-prices. If a brave gave a few of

Horses can carry a good deal more weight than dogs, and the travois was quickly modified to fit the larger animal. The horse on the right is carrying saddlebags and pulling tepee poles instead of a travois.

Horses were often elaborately painted and decorated by their owners. The owner would follow his own taste in decorating his horses, much like the modern car owner paints and decorates his vehicle in a unique style.

his finest horses to a visitor, it was an impressive gesture of great wealth, akin to burning currency or leaving a $100 tip in contemporary American culture. Wealthy Blackfeet by definition owned many horses, while poor Blackfeet owned few or none and often had to borrow horses in order to hunt.

A horse became the brave's most valued hunting companion and was often painted to match the body or facial paint of its owner. A horse who hunted well with his master was revered and cared for even more than the man's wife or wives—after all, a good hunting horse

ensured a good supply of meat for the tepee, and the more meat a hunter could bring home, the more wives he could support. If it was rumored that horse thieves were around, a warrior's buffalo-hunting horse would sleep in the tepee with its master, while the warrior's wife or wives slept outside. Horses who were killed in service to their master were often memorialized in carvings or paintings.

Horses were believed to have souls that lived on after death, and horses who survived fierce battles or seemingly mortal wounds were believed to have strong supernatural powers. There was even a horse cult that was founded by a man who had been shown dances and medicine in a dream by two of his horses; cult members were believed to be able to heal both people and horses, to alter the weather, and to influence the movements of the buffalo. Dying Blackfeet could request to have their favorite horses sacrificed after their death so that their spirit would have reliable mounts in the afterworld. The horses to be sacrificed would be painted with scenes depicting their owner's exploits, then shot in the head at close range near their owner's grave, releasing the horse's spirit near the place of their owner's spirit. (The resulting body could be disposed of in any manner and was not interred with that of the owner.) A poorer family might "sacrifice" the horse by simply clipping his mane and tail, just as a mourning wife might cut off all her hair. The horse was then recognized as being in mourning for its owner (although it was not allowed any respite from work).

Perhaps the most important effect of the horse from a historical standpoint was the way it massively increased the military power of the Blackfeet, enabling them to make frequent, lightning-quick raids on other tribes (albeit they were now subject to such raids themselves).

The Blackfeet could go to war against more tribes and tribes that were quite far away. Elderly Blackfeet interviewed in the late 19th and early 20th century recalled being at war with eight or nine tribes at a time, and mounted warriors regularly crossed the Rocky Mountains to the west and traveled as far south as Utah to attack enemy tribes. Horses not only increased the Blackfeet's military might, they made war all but inevitable. Horse raids against another tribe were viewed as tantamount to a declaration of war, and according to anthropologist and historian John C. Ewers, "the horse raid offered young men of poor parents their best opportunity for economic security and social advancement." Consequently, many attempts at peace negotiations (generally made by older chiefs who were already wealthy) failed due to horse raids made by younger men who were trying to establish themselves.

Although horses had a major impact on Blackfeet culture, their influence was a reflection of the singular importance of the buffalo to the survival of the Blackfeet. The buffalo remained not only the primary means of livelihood but the very foundation and symbol of Blackfeet society. As long as the buffalo was populous and free to roam the plains, the Blackfeet could be assured of their own prosperity and freedom. ▲

A Blackfeet child, sticks in hand, navigates the brush in a pair of leggings made from trading blankets.

THE
LIFE
OF
THE
BLACKFEET

Given the pivotal role of the horse and buffalo in Blackfeet society, it is not surprising that hunting, horseback riding, and fighting skills were considered essential. Consequently, boys were taught rudimentary hunting skills at a young age and played hunting games with their peers that involved stalking each other and dodging lances and arrows. Later, they were taught more sophisticated skills by their elders such as how to track game, how to be brave, how to endure physical pain and hardship, and how to be alert to signs from both the physical and the spiritual worlds. To help them develop these skills, older boys and young men were encouraged to sit in on the conversations of their elders in order to listen and to learn. Girls' education also began early in life, but instead of being trained as hunters, they were trained in their important role as preparers of food and clothing. They learned how to sew moc-casins, how to do embroidery and bead-work, how to cook, and most importantly, how to dress game and tan hides.

Young men went through a number of ceremonies marking the various stages of their development in their effort to become both a hunter and a warrior. One of the most important was the vision quest, a rite of passage that marked the end of their childhood and the beginning of life as an adult. A young man would first meet with a special council of elders, who would advise him on how to go about his vision quest. Then, the candidate would undergo purification by fasting, a sweat lodge ritual, and bathing, all of which were surrounded with prayers and the burning of sweet herbs. The council of elders would then perform a ceremonial dance to ensure protection for the young man while he was alone in the wilderness.

The young man then left the tribe

Blackfeet women and men went on vision quests to mark their maturation into adults. The quester would go off to an isolated area for a few days and wait for a vision to appear. Although visions were considered important, a person who did not have one was considered merely unlucky, not cursed or unworthy.

and found a special place relatively far from the tribe's camp where he would be alone. In order to free his mind and spirit from physical concerns, he would go without food, water, or shelter from the elements. During this time, usually four days in duration, he hoped to see a vision that would provide him with his own personal medicine. A vision might be the sighting of a bear, the hearing of words whispered on the wind, or the sighting of a strange flash of light in the night sky. Whatever vision the young man experienced would become his symbol and part of his personal medicine throughout the whole of his life. Although women did not go to lonely mountaintops as men did, they did pursue their own version of the vision quest, and their visions were taken just as seriously as those of the men. A woman would purify herself in the sweat lodge, usually with the help of several other women, then would go alone to a nearby valley or a small hill in search of a vision.

Young men who were about to become warriors had a special role in the annual Sun Dance ceremony. The Sun Dance ceremony was a lengthy, ornate affair that was considered the highest form of thanksgiving and sacrifice, in which the entire tribe would participate. It was generally performed in the late spring or early summer during a full moon and was sponsored by a different woman each year. Usually the sponsor was a woman of high standing in the tribe who, earlier in the year, had asked the sun to grant her a favor. If the favor had been granted, the woman sponsored the Sun Dance to repay the sun. The sponsor became the Sacred Woman of the Dance and had to fast for days before the ceremony. During the dance, the Sacred Woman would wear a special Sun Dance headdress, a robe of elk skin, and a dress of antelope and deer skins, and she would be treated with deep respect throughout the ceremony by everyone in the tribe. The Sacred Woman would also give away a number of horses during the ceremony, making the dance an expensive one to sponsor.

The ceremony would begin with a plea to the Sun God for the recovery of the sick, which was followed by a period when the entire tribe would fast and pray for their healing. Established warriors would fast and wound themselves as a sacrifice to the sun in repayment for the times they had been rescued from danger. After the fasting and the self-mutilation of the older warriors, the tribe would join together in feasting and joyous celebration, wearing their best clothes, riding the horses of which they were most proud, and asking special favors of the Creator.

For young warriors-to-be, the Sun Dance was a time to prove their courage. These men would first gather branches to build a frame for a sweat lodge—a ritual in itself, with the branch bearers first singing and dancing around the tepee of a medicine woman. Then they would purify themselves in the sweat lodge, while older warriors stood in a specially erected Sun Dance Lodge and told stories of their exploits. Then after

A young man performs the Sun Dance in this 1892 photograph. The Sun Dance ceremony was considered one of the most important ceremonies of the year, allowing tribe members to sacrifice and give thanks to Creator Sun for his beneficence.

a time of fasting and purification, the young men, ceremonially painted and prepared by their Sun Dance sponsors, would enter the Sun Dance Lodge to begin the actual Sun Dance. They would wear necklaces made of bone beads on a band of hide or beaded necklaces with weasel skin hanging from them. They also wore a special cloth which hung from the waist to the ankles, and, according to some accounts, had sage wreaths on their heads.

The dance itself was extremely pain- ful; withstanding it without fainting was a sign of excellent physical endurance. One person at a time performed the dance. The dancers' chest or back skin was pierced with a wooden skewer and attached to a hide thong; the thong, in turn, was attached by a rope to the center lodge pole. The dancers would swing, dancing on their toes, pulling against the thongs of the skewers. While dancing, they would focus their attention and energy on a sacred medicine bundle tied at the top of the lodge pole and would

Two Blackfeet women, Mrs. Henry Standing Alone and Mrs. Bob Black Plume, participate in the ceremonial transfer of ownership of a special type of tepee known as a yellow otter tepee. In their hands is the otter flag, which accompanies this tepee. Painted images of the otter are visible on the tepee liner to the right of the two women.

Blackfeet tepees were painted both outside and in with depictions of visions, sacred animals, the land and sky, or a warrior's achievements.

blow whistles made from eagle bone, the sound of which would be heard by the Great Spirit. Any visions that came to a dancer during this ordeal were considered especially holy and meaningful. The dancer was accompanied by a helper, who aided him in preparing for the dance and gave him encouragement during the dance. Sometimes a young woman would be allowed to give the dancer a bit of chewed herb to renew his strength. Because of the body weight pulling on the skewer, it would eventually rip free from the flesh, ending the dance. The flesh torn from the dancers' bodies was left at the base of the center lodge pole as an offering to the sun.

After the Sun Dance, people were encouraged to give gifts to the poor, and sometimes chiefs gave new names to warriors who had outdone themselves in battle. New chiefs were appointed if replacements were necessary. The entire Sun Dance ceremony lasted about ten days.

Once a man had been to war or taken part in a successful horse raid, he was considered a warrior and worthy of a wife. When a man wished to marry, he would have a friend or relative bring a gift of horses to the lodge of the prospective bride's family. If the woman accepted the proposal, she would feed or water the horses or let them mingle with her father's herd. If she rejected the suitor, she either ignored the horses or had them returned to him. Sometimes marriages were arranged, and in any case the prospective groom usually knew what the woman's response

would be, so the giving and receiving of horses often were simply a formal token of the engagement. The wedding would take place soon after the woman accepted the horses, usually within a few days. The bride left her family's tepee and came into her husband's lodge, accompanied by gifts, personal possessions, and horses that equaled or exceeded the groom's in value. Some accounts maintain that the marriage was formalized by the cutting and uniting of the couple's fingers, so their blood would mingle, symbolizing that they were now one flesh. There was always a big feast after the wedding.

In addition to the large, ornate religious ceremonies that marked important phases in a person's life, smaller ceremonies surrounded everyday activities such as eating, smoking, and hunting. The Blackfeet felt that the flora and fauna surrounding them had spiritual powers and shared a sort of kinship with humans, since all living things were made by the same creator. This respect for things from the earth extended to the animals they killed for food and even the roots and berries they ate and used in their food and medicine. Consequently, religious ceremonies were not relegated to one day of the week, but occurred continually throughout each day to honor and appease the spirits of the living things used. These ceremonies had to be faithfully and exactly executed to ensure success (especially during the preparation of hazardous undertakings such as a battle or a hunt), otherwise the spirits would be displeased, and the entire tribe could suffer as a result.

Not surprisingly, many animals in addition to the buffalo had places of importance in Blackfeet religion. Bears were revered because they were believed to have the ability to heal themselves when wounded and to be invulnerable to other animals' attacks. Wolves were considered highly intelligent; consequently, reconnaissance scouts in a war party wore wolf skins as special medicine. The butterfly was thought to bring sleep; a mother would sew up a piece of hide to resemble a butterfly and tie it in her infant's hair at night to ensure a good night's rest, and tepees were sometimes painted with a butterfly symbol in order to bring on powerful dreams.

Nonliving things also contained spiritual importance. The wind was considered a special messenger of the creator, who would send words of wisdom to the people through it. The circle was believed to best represent the life cycle; consequently, tepees had circular bases, and ceremonial dances followed a circular path (usually in a clockwise direction). The six directions—sky, earth, north, south, east, and west—were believed to have various attributes, and the most revered of these directions was the east, which was the place of the rising sun and thus the place of the origin of life.

One means of honoring the diverse powers inhabiting the Blackfeet spiritual world was through smoking pipes filled with *kinnikinnick,* a mixture of various dried barks, herbs, and tobacco. Smoking was done to protect the smoker from evil, attract game, invoke a spiritual blessing, or seal a pact. A special pipe called a *calumet,* or peace pipe, was smoked at the agreement of treaties and was carried by messengers of peace from one tribe to another. Special medicine pipes, which were used to cure sickness or to bring peace and prosperity to the tribe, were also called Thunder's Pipes, because it was believed that Thunder had given the pipe to humanity. Pipes were decorated in elaborate ways and always treated with great reverence. Eagle feathers were used to decorate pipes because eagles flew very high and very close to the life-giving sun and were consequently believed to be a mediator between the people and Creator Sun. Sometimes the entire eagle was used to wrap the pipe to give it extra power.

The tobacco smoked in the pipes was the sole plant cultivated by the Blackfeet. Tobacco was viewed as a holy and magical plant, and its cultivation was part of a sacred ceremony, surrounded by elaborate taboos, rituals, and beliefs. Tobacco seeds were planted when all the bands of a particular division camped together, then were abandoned but not forgotten when the bands split up. The division would reunite in the area when the tobacco was ready to harvest (the plants were supposedly tended by magical beings in the meantime), and the harvest would be distributed among band members.

Symbols were believed to have a very real power to protect and aid a person; consequently, the designs that cov-

Not all Blackfeet paintings were symbolic; some recorded raids, battles, or legends. Here a Blackfeet man uses pictorial writing to depict a historical event on a hide.

ered Blackfeet clothes, faces, bodies, and armaments almost always contained significant symbolic value. Men's painted bodies often reflected their accomplishments in war or the hunt; for example, if a warrior killed an enemy in hand-to-hand combat, he might paint a hand on each of his shoulders to symbolize his victory. Before going out to hunt or fight, men would often paint protective symbols or scenes outlining a successful expedition on their bodies. After a victorious battle, Blackfeet warriors painted their faces black to indicate their success.

A group of Blackfeet sport a variety of feather and horn headdresses. The upright feather headdress worn by the man on the left, the man third from left, and the man second from right is a style characteristic of the Blackfeet.

Painting the face and body had practical as well as symbolic use, and everybody wore some form of paint everyday, most commonly painting their faces red. In the summertime, the paint served as a sunscreen, while in cold weather, the paint protected the skin from the cold and from chapping. (Much of the protection against the cold came from the layer of bear or buffalo grease that the Blackfeet applied to the skin when preparing it for painting.)

Shields carried into battle were often adorned with the image of an animal who had come to the shield's owner during a vision quest. If, for example, a man had envisioned a turtle during his vision quest, then it was believed that the spirit of the turtle would look after and protect that man. Consequently, he would paint a turtle shell on his shield to ensure good fortune in battle. War bonnets were also frequently decorated with the fur or feathers of animals that had appeared in the wearer's visions. Certain talismans would help the hunter or warrior even if the animal represented had not been a part of his personal vision quest, and experienced hunters often gave useful talismans to younger men. One common talisman was made out of a stuffed kingfisher; since the bird symbolized agility and speed, warriors believed this charm would help them avoid enemy arrows.

Lodges were also painted with symbols. Often, the base was painted red to symbolize the earth, and within this red there would be unpainted orbs to represent stars. Next, the lodge painter would add hills or peaks, with the top of the lodge painted black to symbolize the sky at night. Tepees were often painted with geometric borders on the top and bottom and then decorated with designs which told of the exploits of the tepee's owner. A Blackfeet warrior with an exceptionally illustrious record would paint his tepee liner with pictographs commemorating his accomplishments.

The adornment of clothing was considered so important that the maker would often seek a vision or some other sort of sign from the spirit world for inspiration. Men's clothing was decorated with symbols of prowess in the hunt or in battle, while women's clothing—which was not permitted to bear realistic scenes—was decorated with geometric designs. Most clothing was made from buffalo hide (although in the late 18th century, when trade began with the Hudson's Bay Trading Company,

clothes were sometimes made from the company's colorful blankets) and was decorated with porcupine quills and corn husks that were colored with vegetable dyes and sewn onto the hide. Fringes were made by cutting extra hide at the seams into strips, and pendants, sometimes made from deer toes, were hung onto the clothing.

For special occasions such as important religious ceremonies, men would wear shirts made from bighorn sheepskin, which was soft and white. These shirts were so ornately decorated that they could not be washed and were simply painted brown or red when dirty. War shirts were also made of special hide, usually deer or antelope, and had full sleeves with a fringe of some skins hanging from them. Not only did specific outfits have meaning, but the way in which clothing was worn indicated a certain feeling or intent. A young man courting a bride would wear his buffalo robe over his head, while an older man carried one end of the robe in his left arm, with his right arm unencumbered. During ceremonies, women covered their heads with their robes.

The Blackfeet also made hats from fur or bird skin for use in cold weather. In addition to this practical head wear, fancy headdresses were worn during special events. During victory parties or warrior society meetings, Blackfeet men wore full feather headdresses. Blackfeet women also wore headdresses during special occasions, most notably the Sun Dance when the Sacred Woman of the Dance wore a headdress made of a headband adorned with beads, quills, and feathers and having two long feathers pointing up on either side and a dozen or so animal tails hanging down from it. The sponsor had to buy this expensive headdress from the previous Sacred Woman of the Dance and keep it until the next Sun Dance.

Unlike some other Plains tribes, the Blackfeet usually grew their hair long. Both men and women washed and brushed their hair often and waxed it with buffalo fat to make it shine, but while Blackfeet women simply parted their hair and wore it in long braids, Blackfeet men had much more ornate hairstyles. Men wore bangs and adorned their hair with feathers or quills, while medicine men sometimes coiled their hair around their forehead so that it stuck out like a horn; this unusual hairstyle indicated their position within the tribe.

In addition to clothing and head wear, animal products were used to make tools and decorations. A porcupine's tail made a fine hairbrush, and its quills were used as paintbrush handles as well as ornamentation for clothing. Bear, otter, deer (especially does), coyote, lynx, and wolf were prized for their fur and skin, and their hides were used in clothing, weapon, and tepee ornamentation and the making of drums or headdresses. Elk antlers were used as bows to play fiddlelike musical instruments, with horsehair being used for the strings. The more northern Blackfeet hunted moose, while those located higher in the Rocky Mountains hunted wild sheep and mountain goats for food, clothing, and tools. Beaver pelts became a valuable trade commodity as European traders began to infiltrate Blackfeet territory; as a result, the beaver was hunted to the brink of extinction by whites and Native Americans alike. Later, similar overhunting was to occur with the buffalo.

Not all tools came from animals; stones were frequently used as weapons and as mortars and pestles used for making pemmican. Hot stones were used in cooking dishes such as stews. Most food was cooked inside a cooking bag made from the stomach lining of a large animal such as a buffalo, which could not be directly exposed to fire; heated stones would be placed in the stew itself in order to heat the dish. Heated stones were also placed in sweat lodges, where water would be poured over them to create steam. Wood also had a great variety of uses; wooden sticks were used as stirrers during the preparation of meals, as pegs for piercing and stretching hides, and as frames for tepees, travois, sweat lodges, and bull boats (bowl-shaped vessels made of hide over a wooden frame that were used to ferry people and supplies across rivers). Wood was also used for cradle-boards and was bent into the cagelike structure that was placed on a travois in order to transport children. Stout tree limbs were carved to make the handle for a quirt, which was a combination wooden war club and rawhide horsewhip. Grasses, reeds, and vines were made into baskets for carrying babies and supplies.

The staple of the Blackfeet diet was buffalo meat. After a hunt, the women would roast large pieces of meat on skewers hung over the flame from a tripod. Small bits of meat were cooked in a pot with wild roots and vegetables to make stew. Intestines were cleaned out and stuffed with a mixture of meat and wild sage and onion, making a kind of sausage. Bones that could not be used for other purposes would be broken and added to stew to make use of their marrow.

The Blackfeet varied their buffalo meat diet with other animals such as deer, antelope, quail, and rabbit—but not fish, which for reasons unknown was taboo. The women supplemented the meat by gathering and preparing wild herbs such as sage; vegetables such as wild peas and prairie turnips; and wild fruits such as berries, persimmons, and chokecherries. Prickly-pear cactus, milkweed buds, and rosehips were used in buffalo stew. Other vegetables were obtained by trade with the Mandans and Pawnees, who cultivated and sold beans, corn, squash, and pumpkins. Blackfeet women could preserve food for times of famine by making pemmican or by making a cache, which was a stash of food buried in a large hole in the ground.

The Blackfeet lived well off their land, efficiently utilizing the natural resources available. Their nomadic existence, considered "backward" by white observers, was well suited to the climate and conditions of the northern Great Plains. Likewise, their social and political organization was suited to their nomadic condition and enabled the Blackfeet to flourish on the harsh plains, and, not incidentally, to become an important military power in the area. ▲

Weasel Tail, a Peigan warrior who fought in battle alongside his wife, Throwing Down. Gender and class restrictions in Blackfeet society were quite flexible, and capable individuals could almost always obtain positions of honor within the tribe.

THE
SOCIAL
STRUCTURE
OF
THE
BLACKFEET

One notable element of Blackfeet society—in stark contrast to the norm in Europe and even in the United States of the 18th and 19th centuries—was the flexibility of rank in the tribe. Any man, regardless of birth, could attain a high social rank, provided he lived according to the spoken and unspoken laws and spiritual guidelines that governed the tribe. In addition, a man could govern only with the consent of the people over whom he presided for as long as was thought fit. For example, a chief usually simply retired around age 40, when his physical prowess began to wane; he did not have to be forced out or overthrown. A new chief would then be chosen by consensus.

The structure of divisions and bands within the tribe was similarly flexible. Although the three divisions within the tribe remained the same, the divisions were linguistically and culturally identical, engaged in frequent friendly interaction, and were close allies during any hostilities. Each division was made up of several bands, which were groups of individuals that varied in size. Band structure was extremely loose; although a person usually belonged to their father's or husband's band, this was not always the case, and a person could leave one band and join another at will. Indeed, band members were frequently not related by blood, and although the Blackfeet had a strong incest taboo, marriage within a band was permitted. The bands usually grouped together according to their division during activities such as the Sun Dance or the buffalo hunts, but at other times each band would go its own way to hunt and travel.

The Blackfeet were not governed by

one chief, but instead different bands were each overseen by their own chiefs. Sometimes a council of chiefs would gather for important decisions, such as when considering a treaty, but no chief was officially more powerful than another, and a chief who did not agree with a decision was free to ignore it. New bands could be formed at any time; a man with sufficient standing to become a chief would sometimes simply move away from his old band, and whoever followed him became part of the new band. To attract followers, a would-be chief needed to be a leader in war, in the hunt, and in religious life; in addition, he had to be a charitable and generous man. These characteristics were considered important because it was believed that the nature of the band followed the temperament of the chief. If he was just, calm, and wise, so were his people; if he was not, his band would cause trouble.

Blackfeet bands had war chiefs, who planned battle strategy and led warriors during times of war, and peace chiefs, who settled disputes and set policy during times of peace. Peace chiefs also kept a yearly record of events called the Winter Count. Each year, an event that affected the band as a whole would be recorded, or if no major event had occurred, a remarkable personal event would be recorded instead. Sometimes the Winter Count was kept in pictographs painted on hides, but most commonly it was a verbal record that was memorized by the chief. A few of these were recorded by historians in the late 19th and early 20th century, and when compared against written records of the same period, have demonstrated a remarkable accuracy.

Despite the chief's role as leader, the judicial system under which the Blackfeet lived was usually administered by someone other than the chief. This judge would direct or approve a punishment, which was then meted out by a special council or by relatives of either the wronged or the wrongdoer. Loyalty to the tribe and tribe members was considered tantamount; the punishment for anyone accused of disloyalty to the tribe was death on sight. Crimes against other people were punished severely; someone who murdered another tribe member could be punished by death, and a woman who committed adultery could have her nose cut off. Crimes against property, however, were treated more leniently; in cases of theft, the stolen property was simply returned to its rightful owner.

Order was kept with the aid of the Blackfeet warrior societies. These societies punished offenders, protected the tribe, and presided over organized raids and hunts. The societies were only open to men, and most of them only accepted members from a certain age group. For example, young men who had gone on a vision quest and had participated in a horse raid joined the Doves, while warrior candidates were members of the Mosquitoes until they had proved themselves in battle, at which time they could join the Braves. Generally speaking, societies made up of older, more experienced warriors were more venerated and respected; these included the Bulls and the Brave Dogs.

Other types of societies also existed, with various functions and requirements for membership. Police societies were temporary societies that drew their members, usually younger men who still had to prove themselves, from the warrior societies. They were organized for special functions where a number of rival bands would be present, and they helped to keep the peace. Religious soci-eties had tightly restricted memberships and performed serious ceremonies, such as the secret, sacred rituals performed during the Sun Dance ceremony by the members of the Horn Society. Their activities were held in conjunction with the only women's society, the Buffalo Bull Society; both societies were so prestigious that they had their own lodges for special religious rites during the Sun Dance ceremony. Unlike religious soci-eties, dance societies such as the Kisapas, or Hair Parters, were loosely organized

The women of the Buffalo Bull Society prepare their ceremonial lodge for the Sun Dance ceremony. This religious society, the only Blackfeet society open to women, holds its ceremonies in concert with those of the all-male Horn Society.

A Blackfeet holy man, dressed in an ornate costume, performs a ceremony to cure a dying man in this 1832 painting by George Catlin.

and more social in nature. For example, when the Kisapas held their special dance, participation was open to any young man with the appropriate costume, and their dance served mainly to celebrate and honor the generosity, bravery, and military skill of deserving men.

Warriors could move into a more prestigious society by gaining honor in battle. Honor could be gained by undertaking a dangerous activity; this was known as counting coup. The more dangerous an activity was, the more honor was gained by its successful completion. Consequently, killing an enemy in an ambush did not gain a warrior any status, but taking the gun of a living enemy was extremely prestigious. A common form of counting coup was to touch a living or recently killed enemy with a lance, a hand, or a special stick called a coup stick. The enemy was not harmed in the process (although he was usually already wounded), and the more heavily armed and dangerous an enemy was, the greater the regard for the warrior who successfully counted coup against him. Warriors would recount their coups with scrupulous accuracy during the Sun Dance and other gatherings of warriors; a man who exaggerated his exploits was considered inveterately dishonest and crafty.

Men who were of a more spiritual bent than the warriors could become shamans, or holy men, providing fellow tribespeople with physical and spiritual healing. Shamans could never charge for their services, but it was customary for them to receive gifts of gratitude from the families of healed patients. Although white settlers tended to lump together any Native American they saw involved in healing or religious rituals under the rubric "medicine man," there were actually distinct categories of practitioners among the shamans.

Certain Blackfeet acted as physicians, and these physicians further specialized by treating different illnesses. Every person in the tribe had their own medicine bundle, a collection of items that provided protection for the owner. In the event of an illness or injury, the sick person could meditate on their bundle, but if the condition did not improve, a physician was summoned. The physician used many tools to aid in the victim's recovery, and although each physician had their own methods, they often used herbs, incantations, hot baths, dancing, and the shaking of medicine rattles over the sick person's body.

Physicians were constantly on the lookout for new healing herbs, discovering them through visions or by observing activities of animals (especially bears, who were believed to have a special ability to find useful plants). After learning of a plant with special curative powers, the doctors then experimented on themselves or on patients to determine its proper usage. Sometimes they or their patients died as a result of such trial and error, but the medicine used by the Plains Indians in general was skillfully administered and often successful. Indeed, many medicines used today were originally used by

Native American healers.

Blackfeet doctors dressed simply, but they were easily identified by their unique headdresses. These headdresses were made out of buffalo horn, had hair on the front that was dyed in several colors, and had a furlike tail hanging down the back with feathers and beaded disks dangling on its end. In addition to healing people, Blackfeet doctors treated the tribe's animals and also gave charms to warriors before battle to ensure success. Some doctors also made love bundles, which could be worn by a person desiring another's affections as a type of love potion.

If a doctor could not help a patient, a priest or holy man was sent for. If a sick tribal member was in grave danger, the holy man would sometimes have all the tribespeople gather in a circle around the dying one. They would pray, and the holy man would dance, sing, shake rattles holding special medicine, and make the sounds of the animals that he believed would aid him most in an attempt to revive the patient.

Holy men were not only healers or priests, they were prophets who had a much deeper connection with and knowledge of the spiritual world than doctors or ordinary tribespeople. Holy men dressed much more elaborately than doctors, and much of what they did is shrouded in mystery. White people were seldom allowed to view ceremonies involving a holy man, and after one's death, his costumes, which held his personal medicine, were usually burned. Holy men were able to predict

important things such as the location of buffalo, the outcome of a battle or raid, and the approach of danger. They conducted rituals to help solve any number of problems, including finding missing children.

While Blackfeet men acted primarily as warriors, hunters, and to a lesser extent, shamans, women were the primary caretakers of the tribe. They provided and prepared food, clothing, and shelter for the family; bore and reared children; and made sure camp moves came off quickly and successfully. These duties were not seen as drudgery; on the contrary, they were essential for the tribe's survival and Blackfeet women took pride in their skills in these fields. Women who were exceptionally talented in beadwork, quillwork, or painting could attain high status within the tribe.

Because of the high fatality rate among Blackfeet men, women provided continuity for the tribe. Consequently, they were protected during camp moves by being placed behind the men, who would have to face any dangers first (a tradition misconstrued by European observers as a gesture of disdain). The high proportion of women in the tribe contributed to the popularity of polygamy, which became even more common as the introduction of the horse increased the number of wives a warrior could support. Although polygamy was viewed as disrespectful or sinful by European observers, it was considered desirable by women as well as men because a tepee with more than one wife

An elderly Blackfeet woman, Mrs. Two Guns-White Calf, poses with her granddaughter in this 1920 photograph. To this day, Blackfeet women provide continuity for the tribe by passing on traditions, legend, and history to younger generations.

A Blackfeet woman removes the flesh from a hide she has staked out on the ground. Although most women did not hunt or go on raids, their preparation of food and hides was equally important to the survival of the tribe.

could prepare much more food. One woman working alone could dress only 8 or 10 buffalo during a year's time, while six or more working together could dress over 100. Indeed, first wives sometimes asked their husbands to bring another wife into the tepee in order to help her with the work. Often successive wives were sisters of the first, ensuring cooperation in the arduous task of dressing game.

The division of the genders among the Blackfeet was not a firm one. Men often made their own clothing, and older, married women with the appropriate gifts could become shamans.

According to John Ewers, before the 1880s it was common for young, childless women to accompany their men in battle, hunting, or on raids. Although these women primarily performed such essential duties as cooking and maintaining the camp, they also participated fully in waging war and would help herd stolen horses back to their tribe.

If a woman showed talent in making war, riding a horse, or hunting, those skills were cultivated, and some Blackfeet women became famous warriors and leaders of their tribes. One such woman was Elk Hollering in the Water, who was born around 1870 and who, after marriage, went with her husband, Bear Chief, on raids against enemy tribes. She won high regard for her successful raids, especially her horse raids. (It is important to note that stealing was only considered criminal when it occurred within one's own tribe; when a member of a raiding party took an enemy's possessions it was seen as a form of counting coup.) Another woman named Throwing Down fought at the side of her husband, Weasel Tail, for five battles, until the birth of her first child put an end to her career as a warrior. Throwing Down was reportedly very much in love with her husband and went into battle to protect him.

Sometimes a woman who had lost her husband or family members in a battle against an enemy tribe would be included in the next party to attack that tribe in order to obtain vengeance. One such woman was Pitamahkan, or Running Eagle, perhaps the most famous of all Blackfeet women warriors. Just after she married, her husband was killed in a fight against the Crows. Running Eagle prayed to the sun and asked for a way to avenge her husband's death. She was told in a dream to go on a vision quest, so she went to a cave hidden behind a waterfall then known as Trick Falls, near what is now known as Two Medicine Lodges near East Glacier, Montana.

There she had a vision in which the sun told her that if she became a warrior, she would be successful—but only as long as she remained true to her husband's memory. For years, Running Eagle led hunting, raiding, and warring missions. She could outshoot, outride, and outlast most of her male counterparts, and she was even admitted into the ordinarily all-male Brave Dogs Warrior Society. But in 1860, shortly after responding to the attentions of another Blackfeet warrior, Running Eagle was accosted by a camp guard during a reconnaissance mission into an enemy Flathead camp and was shot. To memorialize the young warrior, in 1981 the name of the waterfall where she had her vision quest was changed from Trick Falls to Running Eagle Falls.

Adventurous warriors and hunters like Running Eagle, who dashingly pursued glory and in the process provided their tribe with food, goods, and security, epitomized Blackfeet culture to many white observers. Although obviously many Blackfeet who were equally important to the survival of the tribe were not warriors, the warriors' lethal skills became increasingly important as their territory was slowly invaded by a strange new tribe, a group of men from the East who trapped beaver, shot buffalo, traded strange items, and called themselves Americans. ▲

This 1874 Harper's Weekly *cover portrays a group of white hunters slaughtering buffalo for their valuable hides. This scene was to become increasingly common as whites encroached on Blackfeet territory.*

EXPOSURE TO OTHER WORLDS

The period between 1750 and 1850—that is, the approximate time between the introduction of the horse and the major influx of white settlers onto Blackfeet land—was a period of great prosperity and comparative isolation for the Blackfeet. Although by the early 17th century Spanish explorers such as Francisco Vásquez de Coronado had traveled northward toward the Great Plains (on horseback, of course), their interactions with the Blackfeet were for the most part limited to being the victims of horse raids.

The first white person to have a more nuanced relation with the tribe also gave a firsthand account of the more ordinary interactions between the Europeans and the Blackfeet. David Thompson, an agent from a British trading company known as the North West Company (which later merged with Hudson's Bay Company), lived among a Peigan band in 1787 and witnessed the triumphant return of a raiding party with 12 mules and 30 horses. The party had set out to attack the Shoshonis but, unable to find the tribe, had pressed on for another 1,500 miles looking for a new target. They surprised a group of Spaniards with a long train of pack mules and horses, frightened away the men, and gleefully led the stock back to their camp.

The first American explorers to encounter the Blackfeet very nearly fell victim to horse raiders. Meriwether Lewis and William Clark spent the years 1804 through 1806 exploring the vast area obtained by President Thomas Jefferson in the Louisiana Purchase. During part of the expedition, Lewis and Clark temporarily split up to explore different areas of the Rocky Mountains, and Lewis led a party of four men with horses and supplies up the Marias River. Lewis, who described the Blackfeet as "a strong and honest people," discovered their aggressive side as his party was attacked by eight Blackfeet horse raiders. The Lewis party managed to out-fight the warriors, killing two of them and taking their horses and weapons, but they had to flee the area in fear of pursuit by vengeful Blackfeet warriors.

The 1800s saw an ever increasing number of hostile encounters between the whites and the Blackfeet. Americans had avoided the Great Plains area, which lacks the lush vegetation of the woodlands in the eastern United States and seemed a wasteland to trappers and settlers, who called the area the Great American Desert. But the whites' perception of the area would soon change. Shortly after Lewis and Clark returned to the eastern United States, they visited the city of St. Louis, Missouri, which at the time was home to a large number of fur trappers. Lewis and Clark's descriptions of an area teeming with game—especially the valuable beaver—fired the imaginations and ambitions of the fur trappers and freed the investment capital necessary to finance expeditions. Soon after Lewis and Clark's visit, a large number of trappers set off for the West.

An intense rivalry quickly developed between the Americans and the British who operated out of Canada. Trappers and traders attempted to ally themselves with the various tribes in the area in order to gain access to their land, and many were eventually befriended by tribes such as the Crows, Nez Perces, Flatheads, Mandans, and Sioux. Because of their hostile encounter with Lewis, the Blackfeet remained suspicious of any overtures by whites. Their antagonism was inadvertently exacerbated by one of the first American trappers in the area, a man named John Colter.

Colter was an experienced woods-man who had traveled to the Rocky Mountains as part of the Lewis and Clark expedition, but left the expedition and remained in the unexplored and unsettled territory for the next six years, hoping to make his fortune in the fur trade. In 1808, he managed to convince the Crows and the Flatheads to send several hundred of their members with him to attend negotiations at a small, temporary trade outpost called Fort Manuel. Unfortunately, the Crows and the Flatheads were implacable enemies of the Blackfeet, who were not pleased with the notion of their rivals gaining access to more and better guns, horses, and supplies. Blackfeet warriors ambushed the Crow-Flathead contingency, and in order to retain the allies he had, Colter fought against the Blackfeet.

Colter was wounded in the battle, but upon his recovery he decided to try and gain the confidence of the Blackfeet. He entered their territory in the hopes of meeting peacefully with tribal leaders and making a trade agreement. Hoping to appear as unthreatening as possible, Colter took only one other person with him, a man named John Potts. Upon entering Blackfeet territory, Colter and Potts were promptly captured by a party of warriors—a turn of events that Colter met with aplomb, realizing that captivity might give him a good opportunity to meet chiefs who would be interested in trading with him. Potts, however, was

Meriwether Lewis led the first American party into Blackfeet territory and engaged in the first recorded battle between the two groups when a horse-raiding party attacked his men.

This engraving shows a group of traders on the Missouri River being attacked by Native Americans. The Blackfeet were especially feared by such traders for their consistent hostility.

less collected and tried to escape; when the warriors tried to stop him, he shot one and was immediately killed.

Any hope for a friendly alliance between the Blackfeet and American trappers died with Potts, and things looked grim for Colter as well when the vengeful warrior party decided to engage in a little sport. Stripping Colter naked, they set him loose and chased him on foot across the cactus-covered desert and rocky terrain. Colter proved the swiftest, managing to outrun all but one warrior, who fell just as he was about to spear Colter. Thinking quickly, Colter dispatched the warrior with his own lance, hid himself under a pile of driftwood floating in a nearby river until the other warriors gave up the pursuit, and set out for Fort Manuel, 300 miles away. He reached the fort only a week later—an impressive time, all the more

(continued on page 73)

NATIVE CRAFT NEW MATERIAL

The Blackfeet have a venerable craft tradition. Before trade began with the whites, Blackfeet decorated their clothing, homes, and tools with feathers, fur, elk teeth, cowrie shells, paint, and dyed porcupine quills. White traders brought with them decorative glass beads and brass bells, and the Blackfeet quickly incorporated these new and colorful items into their designs.

The removal of the Blackfeet onto reservations resulted in a flowering of craft production. Prevented from engaging in their traditional nomadic hunter-and-gatherer lifestyle, the Blackfeet now had a good deal more time to dedicate to craftwork. In addition, most Blackfeet were now permanently located close to white traders who could supply them with a variety of adornments. As a result, Blackfeet headdresses, outfits, and accessories became increasingly ornate, decorated with increasingly complicated beadwork.

A woman's leather purse, decorated with small glass beads. The Blackfeet commonly decorated objects with large triangle, hourglass, or diamond designs composed of many small squares.

A girl's hide dress with an ornately decorated yoke. The beads on this dress were sewn in such a way that they resemble porcupine quill designs.

This woman's dress was made from two elk skins sewn together so that the hind quarters formed sleeves. The yoke is overlaid with beads and fringed with brass-colored beads and cowrie shells.

A swept-back or Sioux-style eagle feather headdress, decorated with beads and weasel pelts. The red and yellow tassels on the end of each eagle feather are wisps of dyed horse hair, glued to the feathers with lime plaster. This style of headdress was adopted by the Blackfeet from other Plains tribes in the mid-1890s and could be worn by almost anyone.

A stand-up or Blackfeet-style headdress decorated with weasel pelts and brass upholstery tacks. This type of headdress, which could only be worn by exceptional warriors, apparently originated with the Blackfeet and was believed to have magical powers.

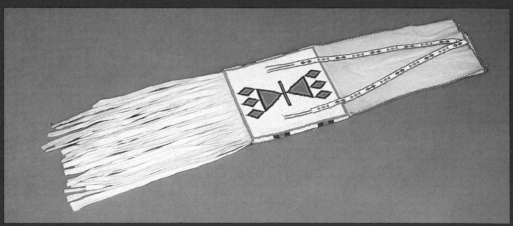

This Blackfeet tobacco pouch was probably used to carry kinnikinnick, *a pipe, and other smoking utensils. Similar pouches were carried by members of almost all Plains tribes.*

69

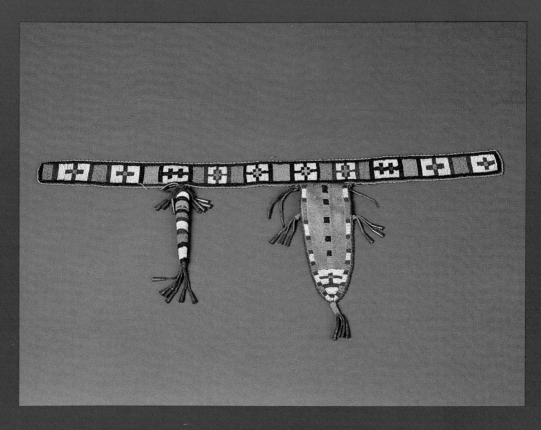

A beaded leather belt with two pouches, a narrow one carrying an awl and wider one for carrying a knife. Metal knives, introduced by white traders, quickly became popular among the Blackfeet, and Blackfeet artisans fashioned many different types of knife sheaths.

Another beaded leather knife sheath, shaped like a beaver.

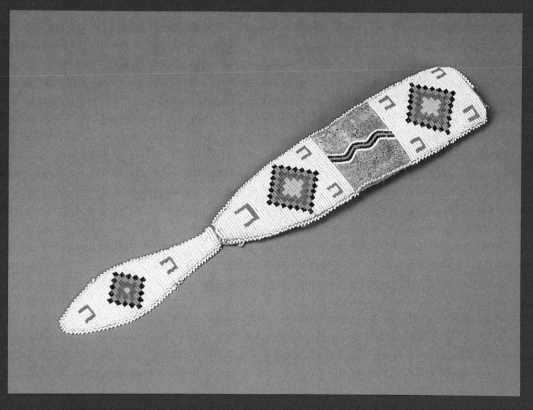

An ornately beaded bodice, beaded to resemble porcupine quills. The bead fringe is decorated with brass bells and cowrie shells.

(continued from page 64)

so considering that he was without clothes, shoes, or supplies.

Colter's second encounter with the Blackfeet simply confirmed their belief that any whites in their territory were a threat. During the 1810s, while other tribes in the area took sides in the British-American struggle for land and power, the Blackfeet attempted as much as possible to keep all whites out of their territory. A resurgence in the British and American fur trades during the 1820s resulted in a new push by trappers to open Blackfeet territory. In 1822, the Missouri Fur Company, which had been forced out of the Three Forks area by the Blackfeet some 12 years before, decided to try again. The company, along with a rival company established by trappers Andrew Henry and William Ashley, recruited hundreds of trappers wanting to reap the riches of the Rocky Mountains. The easiest way to travel into the mountains was to go up the various rivers that flowed out of them, and the canoes and boats of the trappers soon formed a brisk river traffic.

But the Blackfeet were as stubborn and aggressive in 1823 as they had been in 1810—over two dozen American trappers were killed and countless numbers were relieved of their supplies, guns, and furs by war parties. The Blackfeet were especially feared by the trappers both because they were consistently hostile to whites and because their raiding and hunting parties routinely traveled wide distances and never stayed in one clearly defined territory. (Indeed, in at least two cases the Blackfeet forced the abandonment of white settlements established deep within the territory of friendlier tribes.) The trappers quickly abandoned the dangerous river routes into the Rocky Mountains in favor of the less conspicuous overland routes, a decision that was to have egregious effects on all the Plains Indians when legendary mountain man Jedediah Smith led a party over South Pass, a gentle pass through the otherwise rugged Rocky Mountains that was large enough for covered wagons to use. Although it is probable that British explorers discovered the pass before the Smith party, they were the first to pass through it from east to west and to realize its value to settlers wishing to move to the Pacific Northwest. South Pass would eventually form an integral part of the Oregon Trail, the most popular travel route for the flood of settlers who moved west during the mid-19th century.

Although land routes were somewhat safer than the rivers, neither were completely safe, and the fur trappers' insistence upon trespassing in the Blackfeet territory led to vicious consequences. One fur trapper, Henry Vanderburgh, was ambushed, killed, and dismembered by Blackfeet warriors. In a grisly show of bravado, the warriors took Vanderburgh's limbs to Fort McKenzie and defiantly waved them to the soldiers within the walls. British traders also had strained relations with the Blackfeet, mainly because they traded with the hated Flatheads. But in the late 1820s, a former Hudson's Bay Trading Company trapper by the name

A contemporary sketch of a 19th-century Hudson's Bay Company trading post in Alberta that was patronized by the Blackfeet.

of Jacob Berger was able to establish limited trade between the Blackfeet and the British traders. Eventually, overtrapping drove the beaver to the brink of extinction in the area, and by the 1830s, white fur trappers had mostly pulled out of Blackfeet territory.

Blackfeet hostility toward whites lessened somewhat with the departure of the trespassing trappers, and white travelers and traders who were not intent on exploiting Blackfeet land began to receive a warmer welcome. In the early 1830s, Arthur Philip Maximilian, natural historian and prince of Wied-Neuwied in what is now Germany, explored the Great Plains region, witnessing Indian battles and camping and trapping with the Blackfeet. His meticulous notes on his experiences were published in London in 1843, along with the paintings of Carl Bodmer, a painter in Maximilian's entourage. Other artists also attempted to capture what they rightly viewed as a threatened way of life. Alfred Jacob Miller, a Baltimore painter, was employed by the Scottish mountaineer Sir William Stewart to travel with him and to paint what they saw. Miller's paintings of the Teton Sioux, the Wind River Mountains, and Chimney Rock have great emotional depth and achieved great popularity. But the artist who painted the most in-depth and objective depictions of 19th-century tribal life was George Catlin. From 1832 to 1840, Catlin traveled from the Great Lakes region to the Great Plains, visited more than 40 tribes, including the Blackfeet, and painted over 500 scenes depicting virtually every aspect of Native American life.

The 1840s saw the trickle of the white men into the West become a flood. During this period, endless streams of wagon trains filled with hundreds upon thousands of people both from the eastern United States and from foreign countries crossed the Great Plains in what became known as the Great Emigration. These settlers were primarily interested in settling the lands of the Pacific Northwest, but to get there they went along the Oregon Trail, overhunting the area, picking fights with Native American warriors, and permanently disrupting the migration patterns of the buffalo.

Most of this activity affected only the southern fringe of Blackfeet territory, but when gold was discovered in the Rocky Mountains in the 1850s, the situation changed drastically. Immediately, a huge influx of prospectors and settlers moved into Blackfeet territory, and a sharp increase in the number and severity of conflicts between the whites and the tribe followed the migration. The Americans promptly lobbied the U.S. government for protection against Native American raids, and the U.S. government responded with equal promptness, setting the borders of the Blackfeet Nation with the Treaty of Fort Laramie in 1851. The treaty was such only in the loosest sense of the word; the Blackfeet were not present, represented, or consulted during the treaty negotiations or signing. Not surprisingly, the treaty, which also allowed for roads and military outposts to be built on Blackfeet lands, proved impossible to enforce.

The first mutually recognized treaty between the U.S. government and the Blackfeet Indians was in 1855. Called Lamed Bull's Treaty (after a well-known chief of the same name), it stated that the U.S. government would pay the Blackfeet $20,000 per year in goods and services, and devote $15,000 per year toward the "education and Christianization" of the Blackfeet. In return, the Blackfeet agreed to give up half their hunting area and to live in "perpetual peace" with their white neighbors, allowing whites to settle, to travel, and to build telegraphs, railroads, and missions in their territory. Relations improved immediately following the signing of Lamed Bull's Treaty, as the Blackfeet helped white hunters bring down buffalo and traded the hides for wagons, beads, wool, and guns. But before long, whites began to abuse the treaty. The Blackfeet were given spoiled food, broken-down wagons, moth-eaten blankets, rusty guns, and an intoxicating liquid called alcohol that promptly caused a large number of fatalities.

But an even more devastating trend in the 19th century was the near elimination of the buffalo by white hunters. The "immence herds" of buffalo described by Lewis in his journal quickly dwindled in the first half of the 19th century as Europeans developed a taste for buffalo tongue and buffalo hide clothing became the new rage in European fashion. Native American hunting parties frequently discovered huge herds of dead bison with only their tongues and

hides removed—a wasteful practice common to white hunters that appalled the Blackfeet. Even worse, after the transcontinental railroad was built in the 1860s, settlers in passing trains would shoot buffalo solely for sport, leaving the carcass to rot on the plains. This sort of behavior seemed almost insane to the Blackfeet and increased their disdain for and belligerence toward whites.

The situation worsened in the 1860s when white settlers brought great herds of cattle to the former lands of the Blackfeet. These cattle competed with the native fauna for grass, and the practice of fencing off cattle interfered with the migration patterns of the buffalo. The near extermination of the buffalo was assured when in 1860 a German tannery came up with a way to make a refined grade of hide from buffalo skins and industrialists began to use the hide to make machinery belts. The price of hides skyrocketed, and the massacre of the buffalo reached a fever pitch as literally tens of thousands of white hunters swamped Blackfeet hunting lands. By 1883, only a handful of buffalo remained.

The Blackfeet did not placidly accept the reduction of their lands, the disappearance of the buffalo, and the duplicity of the whites. Retaliatory efforts, including attacks on small ranches and settlements, increased throughout the 1860s, and American vigilantes quickly returned in kind. Indeed, hostilities became so common that the Kainah division, which traditionally split its time between what are now Alberta and

The introduction of alcohol to the Blackfeet in the 1850s caused immediate fatalities from alcohol poisoning, violence, and exposure. Traders often doctored cheap moonshine with substances such as ink to make it resemble whiskey, making what was probably already impure alcohol into a truly poisonous mix.

Montana, made the decision to remain in Canada on a permanent basis—as the Siksikas and some of the more northern Peigans had already done. Finally, white settlers appealed to the Bureau of Indian Affairs (which at the time worked closely with the War Department) for redress.

On January 6, 1870, a detachment of U.S. Calvary, led by Colonel E. M. Baker, marched against a band of Peigans in an action known as the Peigan War. The band Baker chose as a target was com-pletely unprepared for battle, having taken no part in raids against the whites and having been recently decimated by a severe smallpox epidemic. In addition, most of the warriors were away hunting, and the camp was primarily composed of elders, women, and children. Nonetheless, Baker ordered a surprise attack, and within minutes, his troops killed approximately 200 Peigans with only 1 U.S. casualty (probably the result of friendly fire). The cruelty of the Baker Massacre (as the Peigan War soon was

Pleasure hunters further reduced the threatened buffalo population. The Blackfeet were incensed at this wasteful treatment of a sacred and necessary animal and soon were at war with the Americans.

called) drew sharp criticism from Congress and the media, but it sufficiently intimidated the Blackfeet into a grudging peace with the intruders. The fatalities of the Baker Massacre were a mere pittance compared to the diseases brought by the continuing influx of settlers—diseases against which the Native Americans had no natural immunity. Smallpox repeatedly ravaged many of the Plains tribes, and the Blackfeet were no exception. In 1837 alone, a severe smallpox epidemic killed approximately two-thirds of the Blackfeet population.

The same year of the Baker Massacre, the area of present-day Alberta, formerly under control of the Hudson's Bay Company, was transferred to the Canadian government in order to open the area to settlement. The government promptly made its influence known by establishing the famous North-West Mounted Police, or Mounties, to keep order in the new territory. Although the Mounties were not the Dudley Do-Rights of popular mythology, their honesty and their respect toward the Blackfeet, as well as their effectiveness in eliminating the whiskey trade in Alberta, won them the regard and cooperation of the Blackfeet chiefs. In 1877, the Canadian government offered to sign a treaty with the Blackfeet that would place them on reservations (called reserves in Canada). Despite the fact that the Canadian officials dismissed any attempt to negotiate more favorable terms, Blackfeet chiefs readily agreed to sign the treaty. Apparently their willingness to sign was motivated more out of respect for the commander of the Mounties, Colonel James F. Macleod, than enthusiasm for or even understanding of the treaty itself. Red Crow, an influential Kainah chief, seems to have summed up the chiefs' thinking when he stated:

> Three years ago, when the police first came to the country, I met and shook hands with Stamixotokon [Macleod's Blackfeet name] at Belly River. Since that time he made me many promises. He kept them all— not one of them was ever broken. Everything that the police have done has been good. I entirely trust Stamixotokon, and will leave everything to him. I will sign.

A letter written in 1879 by an Oblate priest named Father Scollen who was present at the treaty agreement underscores the problems inherent in a compact made between two cultures that lacked any real understanding of one another.

> Did these Indians, or do they now, understand the real nature of the treaty made between the Government and themselves in 1877? My answer to this question is unhesitatingly negative. . . .

> It may be asked: if the Indians did not understand what the treaty meant, why did they sign it? Because previous to the treaty they had always been kindly dealt with by the Authorities, and did not wish to offend them; and although they had

During the 1860s, ranchers brought large herds of cattle into the Northwest plains, increasing the pressure on the buffalo population by fencing off needed grazing land.

many doubts in their mind as to the meaning of the treaty, yet with this precedent before them, they hoped that it simply meant to furnish them plenty of food and clothing, and particularly the former, every time they stood in need of them.

Despite this problem and the fact that the treaty had to be quickly altered to give the Kainahs, North Peigans, and Siksikas their own separate reserves, on the whole the removal of the Blackfeet to reserves was a much more peaceful process in Canada than in the United States. Bloodshed was averted in part because certain prominent chiefs espoused cooperation with the whites and because there was a significantly smaller population of white settlers in the area; but peace held primarily because Canadian authorities wished to avoid the bloody Indian Wars of its southern neighbor, and as a result, were much more likely than their U.S. counterparts to honor treaties and to treat Native Americans with something approaching respect. Relations between the Canadians and the Blackfeet became strained when the dependence and restriction of movement inherent in reserve life became apparent; however, enough goodwill remained that when a number of Native American tribes joined in an armed rebellion against the Canadians in 1885, most of the Blackfeet remained loyal to the crown.

The United States, in contrast, followed what had become its traditional policy of aggressively taking over

The deployment of the North-West Mounted Police into present-day Alberta, Canada, was a decisive factor in maintaining harmonious relationships between the Blackfeet and the white Canadians. Unlike the local lawmen who kept order in the United States, Mounties were generally unprejudiced and fair in their relations with the Native Americans.

Native American land. Treaties signed in 1865, 1888, and 1896, and executive orders signed in 1873 and 1874 moved the southern borders of Blackfeet territory ever northward. Squeezed out, hunted down, ravaged by strange diseases, and deprived of their primary food source, the South Peigans became dependent upon rations provided by the

A group of Albertan Blackfeet chiefs pose with two Canadian officials in this 1884 photograph. Red Crow, head chief of the Kainahs, can be seen standing in the center of the back row.

U.S. government, but this food source proved far from certain. In the winter of 1883–84, the buffalo hunts failed completely, and the U.S. government, in defiance of treaty, failed to provide the South Peigans with adequate winter rations. As a result, over 600 men, women, and children died in what came to be known as Starvation Winter. This tragedy severely weakened the South Peigans and placed them firmly under the control of the only available food source, the U.S. government. In 1887, the General Allotment Act restricted all Blackfeet in the United States to the newly created Blackfeet reservation in Montana. True to form, the U.S. government then demanded further capitulations of territory within the reservation, establishing its present-day boundaries in 1896. The Blackfeet, who were once free to roam an immense territory, were now entirely restricted to reservations and dependent upon governments that were completely foreign to them. ▲

Two Blackfeet children sport fancy traditional garb. Despite continuing hardship and poverty, the Blackfeet have maintained many of their ancestral ways.

THE
BLACKFEET
PEOPLE
TODAY

Shortly after the Peigans agreed to move to a reservation, Congress passed the Curtis Act, which denied tribal governments sovereignty and placed the Native Americans completely and solely under the control of the U.S. government. The act was not aimed at the Blackfeet in particular, but it was designed basically to force all Native Americans to assimilate into Euro-American culture, and it had a detrimental effect on the Blackfeet as well as many other Native American tribes. Under the Curtis Act, Native Americans could be and were forbidden to follow their traditional religion, to speak their native tongues, or to be educated by tribal elders. Even simple ceremonies such as the baby-naming ceremony, in which a newborn is given its tribal name, were banned. In addition, the U.S. government often exercised its control over the Native Americans in demeaning and provocative ways. For example, Blackfeet adults were not allowed to leave the reservation without permission from the Indian agent in charge, nor were any white people allowed to enter the reservation without a pass—and as late as 1908, the Blackfeet reservation was literally fenced in to enforce this policy.

In order to keep the Blackfeet from passing on their traditions to the next generation, children were educated in government-established boarding schools located off the reservation. Many children were forcibly removed from their homes and placed in these schools, and all children in the schools were punished if they were caught singing tribal songs, doing tribal dances, or practicing any aspects of their old religion. Canada's policy toward Native Americans, codified in the 1876 Indian Act, was equally hostile toward native customs, and the Department of Indian Affairs established both day schools on the reservations and boarding schools located off the reservations that were sponsored by the Church of England.

85

Unlike their Montanan counterparts, many Albertan Blackfeet willingly sent their children to the boarding schools, but this was because conditions on the reservations were so harsh that such schools were often the only way parents could guarantee their children adequate food and shelter. Day schools offered no such assurance and thus were quite unpopular.

Although it lacked the missionary forces of the Church of England, the U.S. government did invite many Christian missionaries onto the reservation in the hopes of eliminating traditional (and remarkably tenacious) religious practices. The Jesuits, called "Black Robes" by the Native Americans, had been somewhat futilely involved in missions to the Blackfeet long before the tribe was placed on a reservation. After 1887, the Jesuits became a major force on the reservation, opening schools and teaching the Blackfeet how to raise cattle and how to farm. Perhaps more importantly, the Jesuits learned and preserved the Blackfeet language by translating religious texts into Blackfeet. They also served as mediators between white settlers and the Blackfeet and facilitated treaties on their behalf, but eventually their influence waned as other religions established missions and schools in the area.

Other attempts to force the Blackfeet to assimilate into white culture proved deadlier. Government officials on both sides of the border believed that the Blackfeet should give up their nomadic existence; a 1909 report by the Canadian Department of Indian Affairs claimed that by living in cabins or huts rather than tepees the Blackfeet would be taking "the first essential step towards civilization." Unfortunately, the government did not provide the Blackfeet with adequate housing, and most Blackfeet were too poor to afford anything but poorly ventilated, dark, cramped hovels that proved to be perfect breeding grounds for disease, especially tuberculosis and the eye disease trachoma. Neither government provided its reservations with adequate health care facilities or personnel, and a combination of neglect and poor nutrition ravaged the Blackfeet population. In 1916, one U.S. physician estimated that 64.3 percent of the South Peigans suffered from trachoma while 30 percent had tuberculosis; in Canada the population of North Peigans was halved primarily due to disease between the years 1888 and 1909.

With the extermination of the buffalo, the Blackfeet needed some other form of sustenance. Both the U.S. and Canadian governments provided tribe members with rations; however, these were always at the mercy of cost-conscious government officials. Programs were instituted by both governments to make the Blackfeet economically self-sufficient farmers and ranchers and to lessen their dependence on rations. However farsighted such programs may seem, they often became excuses to cut rations, weakening the Blackfeet, and not incidentally, saving the U.S. and Canadian governments money. For example, rations were with-

Siksika children attend a reservation missionary school in 1892. Such schools were often overcrowded, underfunded, unsanitary, and hostile to traditional Blackfeet culture.

held by U.S. officials during the disastrous Starvation Winter purportedly because the government had already spent money that year on an irrigation project that was supposed to have made the South Peigans successful farmers. Similar policies were followed in Canada, where in the early 1900s an Indian agent gave the Siksikas a onetime gift of

cattle in lieu of yearly rations; when half the stock died in the severe winter of 1906–7, the agent refused to release additional rations, and numerous Siksikas starved.

When economic development programs were not being used as an excuse to cut rations, they were crippled by poor management and unrealistic expec-

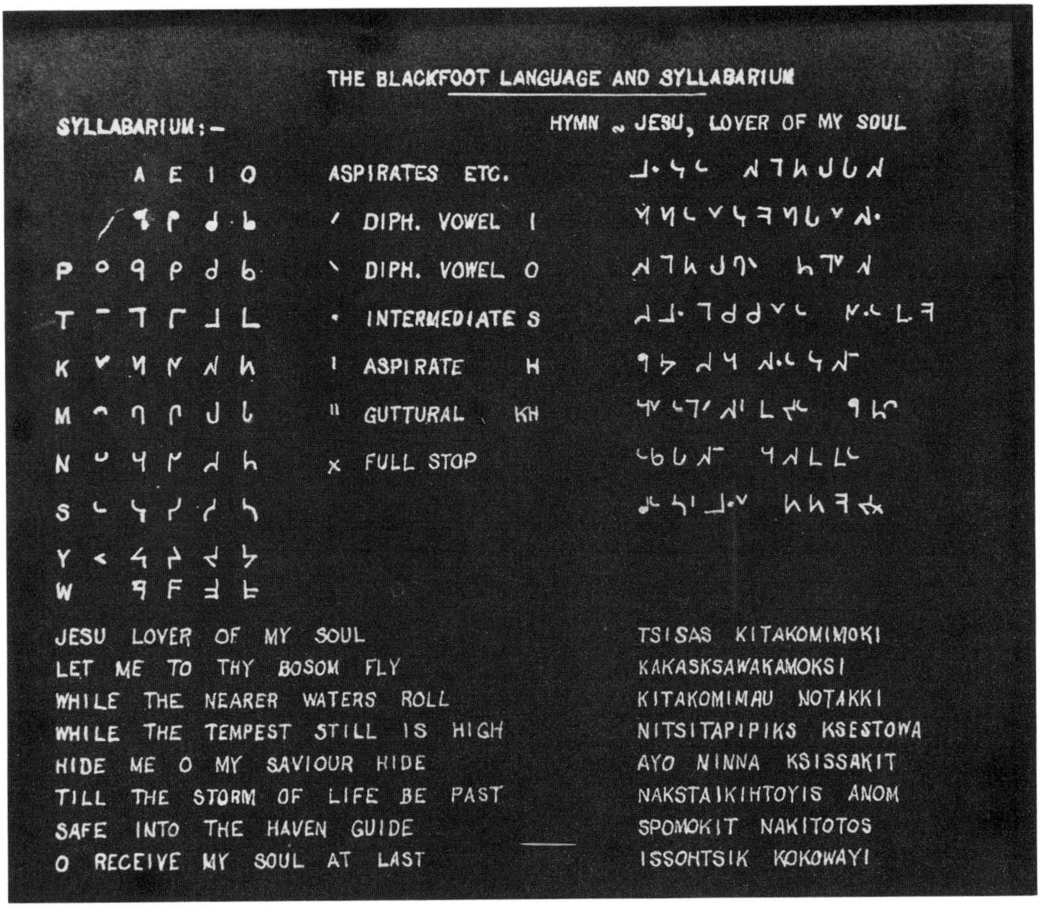
THE BLACKFOOT LANGUAGE AND SYLLABARIUM
SYLLABARIUM:—
HYMN — JESU, LOVER OF MY SOUL
A E I O
ASPIRATES ETC.
DIPH. VOWEL I
DIPH. VOWEL O
INTERMEDIATE S
ASPIRATE H
GUTTURAL KH
x FULL STOP
P
T
K
M
N
S
Y
W
JESU LOVER OF MY SOUL
LET ME TO THY BOSOM FLY
WHILE THE NEARER WATERS ROLL
WHILE THE TEMPEST STILL IS HIGH
HIDE ME O MY SAVIOUR HIDE
TILL THE STORM OF LIFE BE PAST
SAFE INTO THE HAVEN GUIDE
O RECEIVE MY SOUL AT LAST
TSISAS KITAKOMIMOKI
KAKASKSAWAKAMOKSI
KITAKOMIMAU NOTAKKI
NITSITAPIPIKS KSESTOWA
AYO NINNA KSISSAKIT
NAKSTAIKIHTOYIS ANOM
SPOMOKIT NAKITOTOS
ISSOHTSIK KOKOWAYI

Missionaries frequently studied the Blackfeet language to further their own work and to promote literacy. The document pictured here contains the Blackfeet alphabet, a table of characters that represent syllables, and a translation into Blackfeet of the hymn "Jesu, Lover of My Soul."

tations. Most U.S. and Canadian policymakers were agrarian idealists who believed that farming would be a "civilizing" influence as well as a means to economic independence for the Native Americans. Consequently, the U.S. government was attempting to establish farms for the Blackfeet as early as 1855, but this pilot project, along with the majority of farming ventures on both sides of the border, quickly failed. Commercial agriculture was completely alien to the traditional Blackfeet way of life, and the Blackfeet had always chosen their land for its abundance of game and pasturage, not for its quality as farmland. Neither government was willing to fund the necessarily lengthy programs of agricultural education, and while both governments hired men to run educational model farms, these jobs either were doled out to incompetents in return for political favors or were given to men who already had far too many other responsibilities on the reservations to properly tend crops. Finally, the harsh climate of the area made agriculture impractical even for experienced farmers. From 1880 to 1891, more than one million white settlers in the Canadian West found the conditions there so severe that they returned to the better farmlands and milder climates of the East, but Blackfeet who attempted farming were restricted to their reserves and could not move to more amenable areas.

More success greeted attempts to develop cattle ranches on the reservations. The Blackfeet already had a tradition of caring for livestock in the form of horses, and cattle were more rugged than crops and better able to survive droughts and blizzards. In fact, white ranchers had established a booming cattle industry in Alberta by the turn of the century, often grazing their herds (legally or illegally) on the reserves and occasionally losing cows to hungry Blackfeet. But the choice between farming and cattle raising was by no means clear to government officials, who believed that ranching lacked the civilizing influence of farming. As a result, efforts to encourage ranching were relatively intermittent and seriously underfunded in both the United States and Canada. In addition, the Blackfeet on both sides of the border were not allowed to manage their own herds, but had to clear all such decisions with officials. Initially, this policy was enforced to prevent mismanagement of the herds, but government officials were often poor managers themselves, and the policy discouraged Blackfeet ranchers who were never allowed to feel they actually owned their herds. Despite these barriers, by the 1900s the South Peigans and especially the Kainahs were experiencing some success in their attempts to raise cattle.

But a severe blow was dealt the South Peigans when Congress passed the Blackfeet Allotment Act in 1907, which broke up the tribal reservation into smaller units of land that were assigned to individuals. This policy was enacted without the consent of the South Peigans, placing it in direct violation of a treaty agreement reached in 1895, in which the U.S. government promised to never break the Blackfeet reservation up into allotments without the tribe's consent. Some individuals refused allotments, but the Bureau of Indian Affairs assigned them land plots anyway, then opened the "surplus" land—some 800,000 acres—to white settlement.

The land allotment policy was a disaster not only because the Blackfeet in Montana lost hundreds of thousands of acres of land, but also because the allotments themselves were almost useless to the individuals who owned them.

They were too small to herd cattle on, the climate made farming impractical, and the South Peigans lacked the funds to develop the land in other ways. The allotments could easily be sold to non-Indians, and many South Peigan land-owners were swindled out of their land. Due to high rates of illiteracy and traditions that honored verbal wills, written wills were rarely used by the Blackfeet, and in their absence, land allotments were divided among the surviving relatives, resulting in land claims that were too small to support any enterprise and were often sold. In addition, the allotments were taxed, and if taxes were not paid, the land was seized by the U.S. government. The result of these dealings with South Peigan land resources was predictable; a land survey conducted in the late 1930s revealed that sales and seizures of allotments had reduced Blackfeet land holding by 210,000 acres.

Although a form of the allotment system did exist in Canada, Canadian Blackfeet could not sell their allotments to people outside their tribe. In addition, the allotments were not taxed, and reservation land left over after the allotments were assigned remained in tribal hands instead of being opened to white settlement. The entire tribe could agree to sell their land to the Canadian government, however, and the Blackfeet were often pressured both by Canadian officials and their own dire economic conditions into giving up land, usually in return for an increase of rations. Between 1900 and 1920, the North Peigans sold a quarter of their reserve to the Canadian government, while the Siksikas surrendered fully half of their territory.

After the outbreak of World War I, several young Blackfeet men, eager for a means to fulfill the traditional role of warrior, tried to enlist in the armed forces of Canada and the United States but were actively discouraged from doing so by government officials attempting to restrict the Blackfeet to their reserves. As the war continued, the demand for manpower escalated, and some Blackfeet were allowed to enlist and served with honor in Europe. The main impact of World War I, however, was felt on the reservations, where Blackfeet poured money into the Canadian Patriotic Fund and American Liberty Bonds while government officials began drives to increase agricultural output on reservation land to help support the war effort. Such productivity drives resulted in an increase in farming on the Montana reservation that unfortunately proved temporary; on the Kainah reserve, however, the effect of wartime agricultural policy was much more dire. There, agents, given free use of Blackfeet resources and land thanks to wartime directives, neglected and destroyed the profitable Kainah cattle herds during the winter of 1919–20 in what many Kainahs believed was a deliberate attempt to impoverish the tribe and force them to cede territory.

In part to reward Native Americans for their service in World War I, the United States granted Native Americans citizenship in 1924 (Canada did the same in 1960). Citizenship, however, could not

A group of Blackfeet parents confer with their children's teachers in this photograph, taken during the 1910s.

protect the Blackfeet from the oppressive poverty the allotment system was encouraging, so in 1934, the U.S. Congress passed the Indian Reorganization Act (IRA). The IRA ended the practice of giving out allotments, protected Native American territory, allowed tribes to organize sovereign tribal governments, and provided funds for schools, credit programs, and other benefits. The South Peigans quickly took advantage of the new law, forming the Blackfeet Tribal Business Council and writing a formal constitution in 1935. In 1936, Native Americans were deemed eligible for Social Security, allowing elderly and infirm South Peigans access to a reliable source of income. Medical care also improved a great deal in the 1930s, culminating in the opening of a new hospital on the Blackfeet reservation in 1937. Blackfeet agriculture suffered, however,

A Department of the Interior notice advertising the sale of Native American land, circa 1911. The land allotment system, which opened large tracts of Native American land to white settlement, was an unmitigated disaster for all tribes.

as mechanized, large-scale farming became common because Blackfeet farmers generally lacked the funds necessary to purchase expensive agricultural equipment.

During World War II, many Blackfeet men and women served in the armed forces or worked in off-reservation defense plants. Both types of jobs were relatively well-paying, but after the war, Blackfeet workers and soldiers returned to the reservation to discover that a labor glut had further restricted the already limited opportunities for work. Consequently, many people left the reservation in Montana and moved to other western states in search of work. Most of the Blackfeet who left the reservation, however, found themselves working for low wages as unskilled laborers among people who misunderstood and mocked their culture, and many eventually returned. But in the 1950s the landholdings of the tribe eroded rapidly as the postwar population boom among non-Indians created an enormous demand for land in Montana, and Blackfeet who owned or had inherited allotments given out before 1934 sold them to non-Indians. The Blackfeet language was nearly lost as well, as the older Blackfeet who knew the language passed on without teaching it to the younger Blackfeet.

The 1960s and 1970s saw a backlash to this cultural erosion and financial exploitation. The Blackfeet in Montana began actively encouraging elders to teach the old language and the old customs to the younger generations, an effort that culminated in the publication of a Blackfeet dictionary in 1989 and a Blackfeet grammar book in 1991 by the University of Lethbridge in Alberta. Reservation housing in Montana also began to improve in the 1960s and 1970s when several housing projects were developed. The impetus for this development was a disastrous flood that destroyed the homes of 129 families in 1964. The new homes, built with Bureau of Indian Affairs funds, were on the whole larger and sturdier than the old and demonstrated the low quality of most earlier Blackfeet housing. The Blackfeet Indian Housing Authority sponsored projects such as Mutual Help Housing, where people who will be housed in a particular project must contribute their labor to building the project, and no one may move in until the entire project is finished. This work arrangement lowers costs, provides unemployed Blackfeet with the opportunity to learn skills, and helps people build a community rather than merely shelter.

For the Canadian Blackfeet, the 1960s and 1970s were a time of great controversy. In 1969, the Canadian minister of Indian Affairs released the "Statement of the Government of Canada on Indian Policy, 1969," better known as the White Paper, which called for the abolishment of the special trust relationship between the Canadian government and the native peoples living in Canada. Although enactment of the policies outlined in the White Paper would have guaranteed Native Americans civil liberties and autonomy in their financial affairs, it also would have eliminated any special protection of their land. The Indians of Alberta promptly responded in 1970 with a position paper of their own, entitled "Citizens Plus" (also called the Red Paper), which maintained that while the natives of Canada deserved the full rights of citizenship, their status as aboriginal peoples gave them the additional right to claim special protection of their territory. Neither the White Paper nor the Red Paper have been adopted as Canadian policy, which has officially changed little since 1876. As a result, while the Canadian government has ceased procedures such as discouraging native religious practices, it still effectively has complete control over the disbursement of tribal funds, and it has been bitterly criticized for

The British royal family visits the Siksika Reserve in 1939, the year of Great Britain's engagement in World War II. Blackfeet in Canada and the United States supported and fought in both world wars.

underfunding long-term development projects.

The present-day Blackfeet reservation in the United States is located in the northcentral part of Montana, just east of Glacier National Park. It is approximately 2,400 square miles in size and is bordered on the north by Canada, on the east by the Marias River, on the west by the Continental Divide, and on the south by Birch Creek. The political and economic center of the reservation is the town of Browning. Approximately 8,500 Blackfeet live on the Montana reservation, while another 6,500 live in the three Canadian reserves around Lethbridge, Alberta. The Blackfeet, however, are not the only people living on the reservation; many non-Blackfeet Indians and non-Indians live there as well.

As with many Native American tribes, contemporary Blackfeet have been plagued with high rates of alcoholism, suicide, and unemployment, but the tribe is working hard to conquer the problems that beset their community. Alcoholism has been a problem since alcohol was first introduced to the Blackfeet by white traders in the 18th century. The Blackfeet Nation has established alcoholism-prevention programs with the goal of eradicating alcoholism by the year 2000. Programs aimed at young people teach them choice-making skills as well as outdoor and traditional skills in order to kindle their imaginations and to show them they can enjoy themselves without alcohol. These programs are not only run by the Blackfeet but use Blackfeet counselors; as one youth counselor points out, Native American counselors appreciate the spiritual (not necessarily religious) aspects of the harmful effects of addiction:

> What [alcoholism] really does is kill your spirit, and even if you are functioning, you can be spiritually dead. We incorporate Indian spiritual values because the use of drugs and alcohol has brought the People to a level of guilt and shame, and we remind them that the medicine man always says that the altar is always there.

These programs are sorely needed; according to one Blackfeet alcohol-abuse therapist, Fetal Alcohol Syndrome (FAS) occurs in 1 in every 100 births in some Indian communities, and the rate of child abuse in these communities is correspondingly high.

According to U.S. Census figures, unemployment on the Blackfeet Reservation is estimated to be between 55 percent and 64 percent. According to Jim Kennedy, director of revenue for the tribe, only about 2 percent of the people living on the reservation have a college degree, and the percentage of students who drop out of school is high. This is due in part to the fact that agricultural work, which requires little education, has historically been the largest employer on the reservation, providing little incentive for people on the reservation to put time and money into getting a college degree. But the Blackfeet are trying to change these statistics by promoting education and programs to ensure economic opportunities to tribespeople.

Presently, agricultural activities such as farming and raising cattle and horses are still the major sources of income on the reservation, but Blackfeet businesses are growing in number both on and off the reservation. In the past, Blackfeet-owned businesses had a high rate of failure due to heavy governmental regulations, poor planning and management, and a lack of business skills among the Native American population. The Bureau of Indian Affairs, which is supposed to oversee use of the reservation in a trusteelike position, has been criticized for being too controlling and for hampering Blackfeet attempts at both economic and agricultural development. Racism has also taken its toll, both in the classroom and in the loan office. Special loans exist for Blackfeet entrepreneurs, but according to Kennedy, some unscrupulous people "take advantage of their Indian heritage" by lying about their intentions for the money in order to obtain funds. In addition, capitalism—which often emphasizes competition, distrust, and winning at all costs—seems inherently at odds with traditional Blackfeet philosophy, which emphasizes cooperation and mutual trust within the tribe. As a result, many Blackfeet have been afraid that they must betray their values in order to succeed in mainstream American society.

Despite these problems, more business ventures have been succeeding in the past few years. Modern Blackfeet are learning how to function in Western society while remaining true to their own values. The Kainahs in Alberta run a shopping center, a newspaper, and a factory that produces prefabricated homes; and the North Peigans run garment and moccasin factories. The Blackfeet in Montana began a successful reservation-based business with the simple idea of making and selling high-quality pencils, pens, and markers. These writing instruments, made by the Blackfeet Indian Writing Company on the reservation, have been sold in tourist shops, through specialty catalogs, and to businesses for the past 20 years.

The growing popularity of southwestern-style decor has helped spur the growth of the Blackfeet craft industry, and an increasing number of Native American handmade crafts are now sold both on and off the reservation, in shops, and in catalogs. The Indian Arts and Crafts Board, which is a part of the U.S. Department of the Interior, promotes Native American crafts and administers the Museum of the Plains Indian in Browning. The museum, founded in 1941, offers crafts such as pottery, clothing, art, decorative household items, moccasins, shields, and jewelry.

Tours of the Blackfeet reservation are also gaining in popularity. Some travel agencies now specialize in tours of Native American reservations, and the Blackfeet reservation sees roughly two million visitors a year, many of whom also tour nearby Glacier National Park. Although some tourists have denigrating and rigid ideas of what Native Americans are like, most are open-minded, appreciative, and intelligent people who wish to learn about reservation life.

Every site on the tour is full of historical significance to both Native American and white American culture. Tourists can visit the area on the eastern part of the reservation called Ghost Ridge, which contains the communal burial

The Siksika Sun Dance camp of 1943. Despite efforts by government authorities to ban the Sun Dance ceremony, it is still observed, although ritual self-mutilation is now rarely practiced.

grounds of the people who died during Starvation Winter. Chief Mountain, a prominent landmark that was once a sacred site for Blackfeet vision quests, can be viewed looming above Sweet Grass Hills near an entrance to the reservation. Visitors can see Two Medicine River (called the Marias River by non-Blackfeet) near where Lewis had his altercation with the Blackfeet horse-raiding party; the river got its name after two feuding tribes held two separate Sun Dances one year. Tourists can also walk on the Old North Trail, a trail believed to be part of a migration route from Asia that extends from North Canada to Mexico and was used by hunters and war parties in the glory days of the Blackfeet.

Tourists visiting the reservation are sometimes surprised to discover how similar present-day Blackfeet life is to their own. Many Blackfeet are practicing Catholics, Baptists, Evangelists, and Methodists, although some still practice the traditional Blackfeet religion, and

A Blackfeet man tells his son the legend of the peace pipe. The 1960s and 1970s brought a resurgence of interest in traditional Blackfeet culture that continues today.

many combine practices from both religious traditions. They wear modern clothes, eat fast food, and own cars and trucks. There are now several good schools on the reservation, as well as gas stations, grocery stores, hardware stores, and libraries. There is also a community college, which graduates about 35 students annually. Everyone speaks English, and a minority speak Blackfeet as well.

Despite these signs of assimilation, Blackfeet culture is still very much in existence. In his book *Modern Blackfeet*, anthropologist Malcolm McFee describes what he calls the "Third Generation Phenomenon." Despite the pressure to assimilate and the intermarriage between whites and Native Americans, McFee feels that Blackfeet culture will remain strong, because

> the children of white-oriented families
> who have achieved a measure of
> economic security are taking an
> increased interest in Indian
> traditions. . . . College youth who
> have been taken up in the . . .
> student Indian movements . . . and
> their peers on the reservation are
> not only asserting their Indian
> identity, but their tribal identity as
> well.

McFee hopes that the young mixed-race Blackfeet will eliminate the social divisions of the Blackfeet community and will by their very existence bring greater understanding and harmony between Indians and non-Indians. McFee adds that those who are full-blooded Blackfeet Indian and have clung tenaciously to the old ways despite sometimes violent opposition can give these mixed-race Blackfeet a "source of identity and pride" and enrich the quality of everyone's lives.

For the Blackfeet and other Native American nations, the winds of change are beginning to blow in their favor. Native Americans are finding more empathy among the white population toward their past problems and present needs. Young men and women who could not wait to get off the reservation a generation ago are returning armed with college degrees, practical experience, pride in their ancestry, and a desire to help their people. A large part of the current prosperity of the Blackfeet Nation is due to the leadership of the current chief, Earl Old Person. Old Person is a full-blooded Blackfeet who attended school on the reservation and has been involved in Blackfeet tribal government since he was seven years old. He has served for 36 years on the Blackfeet Tribal Business Council (13 of those years as chairman), is the founder and chief executive officer of the Blackfeet Indian Writing Company, and has strongly dedicated himself to promoting Native American ideals and encouraging positive intercultural relations. His effectiveness as a leader has resulted in his being honored by a number of U.S. presidents, the prime minister of Canada, and the Royal Family of England.

One of the most successful efforts of the Blackfeet to revive their old ways and preserve their culture is the annual

Three Kainah children stand in front of a play tepee made of flour sacks. Many contemporary Blackfeet parents now make a serious effort to teach their children to value, cherish, and practice traditional ways.

North American Indian Days celebration, called a powwow. Open to Indians and non-Indians alike, the Blackfeet powwow—held in Browning, Montana, for four days during the second week in July—is one of the largest on the continent. People come from all over the country and the world to watch and to participate in the celebration, camping in recreational vehicles, tents, and even tepees, while engaging in dancing, dance contests, storytelling, drumplaying, and games. Traditional Plains Indian foods such as boiled potatoes, boiled beef and venison, sarvisberry soup, bannock bread (baking powder bread), and fry bread are served.

Besides simply having a good time at these powwows, the Blackfeet hope to promote and instill in mainstream white society a greater appreciation for their culture. The powwow lasts four days, the traditional length of a vision quest, in the hopes that all the people who attend the festival come away with a bright new vision of a future where different cultures and different races are equally appreciated, valued, and respected. ▲

BIBLIOGRAPHY

Dempsey, Hugh A. *Charcoal's World*. Lincoln: University of Nebraska Press, 1978.

———. *Crowfoot: Chief of the Blackfeet*. Norman: University of Oklahoma Press, 1972.

———. *Red Crow, Warrior Chief*. Lincoln: University of Nebraska Press, 1980.

Grinnell, George Bird. *Blackfoot Lodge Tales: The Story of a Prairie People*. Lincoln: University of Nebraska Press, 1962.

Hungry Wolf, Adolph. *The Blood People: A Division of the Blackfoot Confederacy*. New York: Harper & Row, 1977.

Hungry Wolf, Beverly. *The Ways of My Grandmothers*. New York: Quill, 1982.

Lancaster, Richard. *Piegan*. Garden City, NY: Doubleday, 1966.

McClintock, Walter. *Old Indian Trails*. 1923. Reprint. Boston: Houghton Mifflin, 1992.

McFee, Malcolm. *Modern Blackfeet: Montanans on a Reservation*. New York: Holt, Rinehart & Winston, 1972.

Scriver, Bob. *The Blackfeet: Artists of the Northern Plain*. Kansas City, MO: Lowell Press, 1990.

Walton, Ann T., et al. *After the Buffalo Were Gone: The Louis Warren Hill, Sr., Collection of Indian Art*. St. Paul, MN: Northwest Area Foundation, 1985.

THE BLACKFEET AT A GLANCE

TRIBE   *Blackfeet*
CULTURE AREA   *Northern Great Plains*
GEOGRAPHY   *Montana, Idaho, Wyoming, Alberta, British Columbia, Saskatchewan*
LINGUISTIC FAMILY   *Algonquian*
CURRENT POPULATION   *Approximately 8,500 on Montana reservation; 6,500 in Canada*
FEDERAL STATUS   *Tribal reservation near Browning, Montana; three Canadian reserves around Lethbridge, Alberta*

GLOSSARY

agent A person appointed by the Bureau of Indian Affairs to supervise U.S. government programs on a reservation and/or in a specific region.

anthropologist A scientist who studies human beings and their culture.

archaeologist A scientist who studies the material remains of past human cultures.

band A loosely organized group of people who are bound together by the need for food and defense, by family ties, and/or by other common interests.

Blackfeet Allotment Act The 1907 federal law that divided reservation land into small allotments assigned to individual families and sold the surplus to whites. This policy undermined the traditional native way of life.

Bureau of Indian Affairs (BIA) A federal government agency, now within the Department of the Interior, founded to manage relations with Native American tribes.

calumet A peace pipe smoked at the agreement of treaties and carried by messengers of peace from one tribe to another.

counting coup A system of ranking acts of bravery in war.

Creator Sun In Blackfeet mythology, the supernatural being who created the world.

culture The learned behavior of humans; nonbiological, socially taught activities; the way of life of a group of people.

Curtis Act A federal law that placed Native Americans completely under the control of the U.S. government. The law was used to force the Blackfeet to assimilate into white culture, forbidding Native Americans to practice their traditional religion and speak their native language.

esoteric Relating to knowledge restricted to a small, specially initiated group.

Indian Reorganization Act (IRA) The 1934 federal law that ended the policy of allotting plots of land to individuals and encouraged the development of reservation communities. The act also provided for the creation of autonomous tribal governments.

peace chief A respected leader who settled disputes, set policy, and kept a record of the tribe's history.

reservation A tract of land retained by North American Indians for their own occupation and use; called a reserve in Canada.

shaman A holy man who provides physical and spiritual healing for the tribe.

Sun Dance A sacred ritual performed every summer in which the Blackfeet give thanks for good fortune by performing different acts. In the most dramatic facet of the ritual, men pierce their flesh with a skewer attached by a thong to a pole and dance around the pole until they tear free.

sweat bath A ritual purification in a heated lodge filled with steam, often undertaken as preparation for contact with supernatural beings.

talisman An object believed to protect or bring good fortune to whomever carries it. The Blackfeet discovered many of their talismans through vision quests.

treaty A contract negotiated between nations that deals with the cessation of military action, the surrender of political independence, the establishment of boundaries, the terms of land sales, and related matters.

tribe A society consisting of several separate communities united by kinship, culture, language, and other social institutions, including clans, religious organizations, and warrior societies.

vision quest A sacred ritual in which a person, spiritually purified through a sweat bath, went off alone for four days of fasting and praying in order to receive visions from a supernatural spirit who would act as a personal guardian.

war chief A respected warrior who planned battle strategy and led the warriors during times of conflict.

INDEX

PICTURE CREDITS

THERESA JENSEN LACEY, an award-winning freelance writer and journalist, has been accepted to the 1995 *Who's Who in the South and Southwest*. A descendant of Chief Quanah Parker, she was inspired by her Comanche and Cherokee lineage to study Native American history. Lacey currently lives in Tennessee.

FRANK W. PORTER III, general editor of INDIANS OF NORTH AMERICA, is director of the Chelsea House Foundation for American Indian Studies. He holds a B.A., M.A., and Ph.D. from the University of Maryland. He has done extensive research concerning the Indians of Maryland and Delaware and is the author of numerous articles on their history, archaeology, geography, and ethnography. He was formerly director of the Maryland Commission on Indian Affairs and American Indian Research and Resource Institute, Gettysburg, Pennsylvania, and he has received grants from the Delaware Humanities Forum, the Maryland Committee for the Humanities, the Ford Foundation, and the National Endowment for the Humanities, among others. Dr. Porter is the author of *The Bureau of Indian Affairs* in the Chelsea House KNOW YOUR GOVERNMENT series.